The Great Church-State Fraud

The Great

Church-State

FRAUD

C. Stanley
LOWELL

Robert B. Luce, Inc.   Washington-New York

Contents

This book is for my daughter,

Arianne Parker Lowell

1. Church-State Relations: the American Dream

From the days of ancient Egypt until now the interlocking of church and state has been one of the most prolific sources of mankind's ills. Both church and state have suffered immeasurably from this relationship, but the people themselves have been the principal victims.

It was the genius of the American founding fathers to detect this flaw in the all but universal pattern of church-state relationships. Their determination to separate church and state was the direct result of this discovery. Their plan represented a radically new concept of church-state relations though it had been anticipated by the sectarians of the Reformation who had suffered much from both Lutheran and Roman Catholic establishments. Their plan relied on the basic premise enunciated by James Madison in his *Memorial and Remonstrance Against Religious Assessments* that "religion is not within the cognizance of Civil Government." Government should do nothing to promote religion or inhibit religion, nothing to provide for religion, or deprive religion. Religion was not a proper area for government activity. This concept broke sharply with the past when religion had invariably been conceived as a primary concern of government. Under the new plan government was to do nothing where religion was concerned.

The complete text of the First Amendment which safeguards basic liberties of the people from governmental intrusion is as follows:

7

Congress shall make no law respecting an establishment of religion, or prohibiting the free exercise thereof; or abridging the freedom of speech, or of the press, or the right of the people peaceably to assemble and to petition the Government for a redress of grievances.

The capstone of the First Amendment is the religious freedom clauses which the founders properly placed first.

The religion clause was not merely a ban on establishment of religion; it was a ban on *anything respecting this.* Any activity which pertained to this or related to this was forbidden. The policy was adopted not with the idea of reducing or eliminating religion. It was believed that religion would be more virile if left in a free climate without either government sponsorship or interference.

The object of the "no-establishment clause" was certainly not the Roman Catholic Church as has sometimes been suggested. There were no Catholic establishments in the colonies and, indeed, few Catholics. There were fewer than 18,000 Catholics in all the colonies at the outbreak of the American Revolution. But there were Congregational or Episcopal establishments of religion in nine of the thirteen colonies. The First Amendment did not immediately affect these establishments, one of which persisted until 1833, but it did preclude any such development on the national scene. Much later, the First Amendment was to be made applicable to the states by the Fourteenth Amendment.

Not only does the religion clause of the First Amendment protect religion from acts "respecting establishment," it also guarantees "free exercise." Each person is free to profess whatever faith he chooses or no faith at all, without government interference. Religious groups are free to win adherents, organize, collect funds and acquire property. Both individuals and groups are free to do practically anything in the name of religion unless it would violate public health or morals, or infringe upon the liberty of others.

Separation of church and state is functional: It would avoid interlocking of the processes (reciprocal embroilments) of the two. It is also financial. The state will not employ its taxing power on behalf of the churches. Actually, there is no better way to establish religion than to finance it. Government is to avoid this. Indeed, the religion clause itself emerged out of a bitter controversy over state financing of religion in many of the colonies. In a letter to Edward Livingston in 1822 James Madison pointed to the "lesson that religion flourishes in greater purity, without than with the aid of government."[1]

Thomas Jefferson, with Madison one of the great architects of church-state separation, declared in his *Virginia Act for Establishing Religious Freedom* that "to compel a man to furnish contributions of money for the propagation of opinions which he disbelieves, is sinful and tyrannical, that even the forcing him to support this or that teacher of his own religious persuasion, is depriving him of the comfortable liberty of giving his contributions to the particular pastor . . ."

One of the clearest statements of the meaning of separation was made by Justice Black in *Everson v. Board of Education* in 1947. He said:

> The "establishment of religion" clause of the First Amendment means at least this: Neither a State nor the Federal Government can set up a church. Neither can pass laws which aid one religion, aid all religions, or prefer one religion over another. Neither can force nor influence a person to go to or remain away from church against his will or force him to profess a belief or disbelief in any religion . . . No tax in any amount, large or small, can be levied to support any religious activities or institutions, whatever they may be called, or whatever form they may adopt to teach or practice religion.[2]

The genius of the separation arrangement as conceived by the founding fathers is that it removes the element of legal coercion from religion. This has been healthy for religion itself. Nothing more quickly undermines the strength and appeal of religion than to clothe it with the authority of the state and make its demands legally binding on men. It is this that has produced clericalism and fed the fires of anti-clericalism. By divorcing the state's coercion from religion the founding fathers sought to avoid the kind of inter-creedal bitterness which had so often erupted in armed conflict. The arrangement they conceived and planned did succeed in avoiding many of these problems. When James Bryce came in the last century to study the American scene he quickly observed that separation of church and state was one of the secrets of its success. He wrote:

Of all the differences between the Old World and the New this is perhaps the most salient. Half the wars of Europe, half of the internal troubles that have vexed European states . . . have arisen from theological differences or from the rival claims of church and state. This whole vast chapter of debate and strife has remained virtually unopened in the United States. There is no established church. All religious bodies are equal before the law, and unrecognized by the law, except as voluntary associations of private citizens. No attempt has ever been made to alter or infringe upon these provisions.[3]

This, then, is the arrangement that the founding fathers conceived. They believed it would prove healthy both for religion and for the state. Such is separation of church and state as the First Amendment defined it, as the Supreme Court has interpreted it and as most Americans understand it.

Notes

1. *American State Papers.* p.193
2. *Everson v. Board of Education.* 330 U.S. 1 (1947)
3. James Bryce, *The American Commonwealth.* 2nd edition, revised, II p.763

2. Church-State Relations: the Reality

When one examines the contemporary scene in church-state relations what he sees is something quite different from that described in the previous chapter. What he sees is a country where government pours vast sums into church institutions and programs. In several states, despite strict constitutional provisions to the contrary, strenuous efforts are under way to provide tax funds for the direct support of church schools. Some of these "establishments" have been checked at least for the time being by action of the courts and there is some evidence that the tide is turning the other way. But elsewhere dubious subsidies continue and the legislatures of many states feel clerical pressures for similar enactments. Such aids as bus transportation, textbooks and auxiliary educational services are commonly provided from tax funds for these institutions. At the state and local levels much of the welfare program of the church is financed from taxes.

At the federal level, government is providing some financial aid for church institutions in a variety of ways. Among these institutions are elementary and secondary schools, higher institutions of learning, and even parish churches. There are more than 150 programs of aid to education alone and church institutions share in most of them. In the area of health care many millions of tax funds are poured annually into church institutions. Under the Hill-Burton Act which went into effect in 1947 the federal government finances the building of church-related hospitals in many communities, then provides various forms of continuing support. It is

11

interesting and significant that with each renewal of Hill-Burton the religious sector has progressively increased its share of the funds. The public sector, with none to exert political muscle on its behalf, has seen its percentage steadily decline. Education and healing are noble endeavors but under these banners the churches receive government subsidy.

Providing shelter for mankind is another worthy program which touches basic human need. In this category, churches have entered into highly profitable operations — all with government money. While individuals have not profited, their corporations have flourished and the church structure has been sustained. Why should this not happen when church operators can finance their businesses at highly advantageous interest rates via the federal government? Seventy-five percent of housing for the elderly with FHA mortgage insurance is provided by churches and their organizations. Over half of similar projects financed by the Community Facilities Corporation are being built by churches and their organizations. Under the guise of charitable and welfare endeavor the church moves into big business with its capital supplied by the state.

After World War II the federal government found itself with land and other property for which it had no immediate need. Instead of selling the property to bidders to recover a part of its original cost, it was suggested that it be donated to private groups for welfare and education uses. As soon as these surplus properties were offered, churches were at the head of the line. They received highly valuable land, buildings and other property for nothing, or for a small fraction of true value. Churches have also reaped a rich harvest in urban renewal programs which they have frequently exploited to establish themselves via government's eminent domain in highly strategic and desirable situations.

As a welfare adjunct to their missionary work the churches have received many kinds of government assistance. They have been aided in their proselytizing programs by serving as distributors of government goods both in this country and abroad. Their institutions and personnel in the foreign field have been aided in various ways. War claims legislation has been trapped to provide

12

large sums for church institutions. This writer recently attended a Senate hearing where he witnessed a parade of church representatives pleading that their claims should receive top priority in the distribution since it had become evident that there would not be sufficient funds to pay all claims in full. Their argument was that they would do better with the funds than the other claimants. When the decision was made they had their way.

The federal example has stimulated the states. Some of them are similarly pouring tax dollars into church operations and institutions. (Government aid flowing to church schools shall be called "parochiaid" in this work.) This is particularly true in the fields of welfare and education. Local communities also provide some forms of aid for churches. Over all, there is the enormous boon of tax exemption. This applies, of course, to religiously used property and sometimes to other property owned by churches. There is also the exemption from tax on income derived from such unrelated businesses as shopping centers, liquor, gambling, trash collection, hotels, ranches, baked goods, canned goods, electronics, printing, foundation garments, electrical fixtures, parking garages, and many others. It is true that the federal government has moved to lift this exemption, where borrowed money is involved, but it will continue to apply to all existing church-owned businesses at least until 1975.

While the financing of the churches by government is a highly dramatic church-state development, the interlocking of the processes of the two may be even more significant. The fact is that today government regards the church as simply another agency to be used in the furtherance of its social programs. Government hires churches just as it hires many other kinds of private agencies. As it hires the church, the government comes into the church, so as to speak. Inevitably so. For, having hired the church, the government cannot then walk away and forget about it. Like any other manager, government has a continuing responsibility to see if it is getting its money's worth. Government must certainly make its stipulations about the kind of performance it expects and then continue its surveillance to see that this is duly delivered. At least to

13

the extent of the hired projects, government becomes the mentor of the churches, directing them as to what they are to do and how they are to do it. Thus, the church becomes for government an engine of social polity. Under such circumstances, the church's only alternative to being controlled by government is for itself to control the government. History provides its examples of this development.

Today, there is stark contrast between our preaching and our practice. Here, on the one hand, is what our founding fathers bequeathed and what we supposed we had. And here, on the other hand, is something altogether different that we actually do have. On the one hand, separation of church and state with no functional or financial interlocking of the two; on the other, a growing union of church and state with an increasing interlocking of finance and management. The contrast is startling.

How could this have possibly come about? How can we be in fact approaching a practical union of church and state while loudly and even earnestly proclaiming separation of the two? The answer is that this dramatic shift is being accomplished by a series of tricks and ruses which bring vast sums from the state into the coffers of the church and consequent links in management between the two. Some of these devices are so transparent as to be ludicrous. Others are more subtle. But in total, the tricks appear to be enjoying some success. The people become tolerant of a new church-state arrangement without realizing that a change has taken place.

The business of interlocking state with church and taxing for the support of religion has a long and dreary history extending back into most civilizations. The strategy of deceit and circumvention is leading us, step by step, from brilliant success back to demonstrated failure. The ruses are being advanced by masters of deceit who use them to circumvent the constitution, to do by indirection what they may not do directly. The ruses are also employed by well disposed but uncritical people with the same result. Their efforts comprise a massive fraud on the American people. At an appropriate point (Chapter 9) we shall analyze each of these tricks. Here we shall merely identify them.

14

The first and most popular ruse is the so-called child benefit theory that government can provide aid for children in church schools without aiding the schools. The aid is aid to persons, not institutions. Another ruse is that the state can subsidize the secular instruction offered in religious schools without providing any benefit for religion. A third is that since the state imposes certain requirements on church schools — e.g. record keeping — it can provide such institutions funds for the performance of this service. A fourth is that it is cheaper for government to hire the church for certain services than for government to perform the services itself; there are the pleas that the state needs the aid of the church in such worthy causes as buttressing national defense and in winning the war against poverty. There is the appeal for competition in education via government vouchers for parents which are receivable in any school, parochials included, which they may choose for their child. There is the claim that government aid to church schools is not really such if only it is channeled into the institution via reimbursement or tax credits for parents. Also the assertion that government subsidies to parochial schools save the public money. Finally, there is the contention that in advancing the general welfare, government should overlook no group or agency that might prove useful. Churches may be subsidized in enterprises that benefit the general welfare provided only that these subsidies do not aid or inhibit religion.

Under such flimsy banners a mighty establishment of religion is rising. State and church today are like two drunks holding each other up. The church looks increasingly to government for its financing and direction. The state turns to the church as its agent in welfare and education and a bulwark of political support. Clerical opportunists connive with political leaders seeking votes, to perpetrate the fraud. The result is one that mankind has learned to expect from such an arrangement — a church swelling with sterile institutionalism but increasingly devoid of spiritual significance; and a state shorn of the prophetic church when it needs it most. Just how this is coming about today is a story that needs to be told.

15

3.   The Great End Run

During the Presidential Campaign of 1964, Lyndon B. Johnson made federal aid to education one of his big vote-getting appeals. His Republican opponent, Barry Goldwater, did not believe in federal aid. Johnson made the most of the issue. He stressed it time and time again. In a policy paper signed by the President and released November 1, 1964 at the climax of the campaign, Johnson declared: "We must provide a good education for every boy and girl — no matter where he lives."

This was all well and good but it failed to mention the real impediment to federal aid to education which had caused it to fail in three previous administrations. This was the church-state problem — whether church schools could receive a share of federal aid. Significantly, the original version of the policy paper contained a statement squarely in the tradition of former President Kennedy opposing aid to parochial schools. But no reference to this appeared in the final version. Johnson was meeting privately with church leaders during this period and quietly assuring them that he would find a way to aid their institutions along with the public schools without raising the old church-state bugaboo that had defeated the Kennedy program.

For the benefit of the Protestants, Johnson was talking out of the other side of his mouth. When E.S. James, editor of the Texas *Baptist Standard,* asked his views on federal aid to church schools, Johnson replied:

I believe in the American tradition of separation of church

and state which is expressed in the First Amendment to the Constitution. By my office — and by personal conviction — I am sworn to uphold that tradition. Therefore, I would oppose any federal program — including assistance to schools — which does not strictly conform to this constitutional requirement.

The Catholic hierarchy was not dismayed by this statement, however, for it was acquainted with a letter which the White House had dispatched to Citizens for Educational Freedom, one of its action arms, on March 19, 1964. The letter which appeared in the Brooklyn *Tablet* September 17 of that year states:

The President favors appropriate aid (on the principle of equalizing educational opportunities) to public elementary and secondary schools, but would not recommend the inclusion of private or parochial schools because this would violate the Constitutional provisions with reference to separation of Church and State. He hopes that in poverty situations some special aids which do not pertain to religious instructions, for health and nutrition of individual children may be authorized without infringing upon the Constitution.

Here were two kinds of talk which, if not contradictory, were certainly different. This was typical political talk — giving comfort to both sides in the hope of working out an accommodation at least passably acceptable to both. The trouble was that the church-state question in federal aid to education was not an ordinary, horse-trading issue. It was deeply rooted in history and had also figured prominently in the brief record of the American republic.

To understand this we must have a look at the church-state issue as it had confronted previous Administrations. The question of whether or not church schools should be included in federal aid to education had appeared in both the Eisenhower and Truman Administrations, but it was during the campaign and incumbency of John F. Kennedy that it burgeoned into national prominence. At that time the issue was faced openly and candidly. There were special reasons for this.

Kennedy was a Catholic. No Catholic had ever been elected President. There was some apprehension as to what a Catholic in the White House might do on a matter like federal aid to

18

education. For the Catholic hierarchy in the United States had long taken the position not only that it had a right to educate all Catholic children in a separate school system but that government ought to require all taxpayers to pay for this separate system.

Tax support for a separate Catholic school system had been an official demand of the Roman Catholic hierarchy for a long time. In the 1840's Bishop John Hughes of the New York diocese battled for the principle that the Catholic schools should receive their share of the tax funds for the children they were educating. In 1841 Bishop Hughes actually organized a Catholic political party and put it on the ballot in New York. The Catholic party was decisively defeated and advocates of common schools serving all religious groups and supported by public funds emerged victorious.

Though defeated in this and other political battles, the Catholic leadership never abandoned its claims for tax support of its schools. This became evident a century after Bishop Hughes when federal aid to education emerged as a full-fledged political issue. In 1947, the House Committee on Education and Labor held extensive hearings on aid to education. The testimony presented by Monsignor (later Bishop) William E. McManus, the official representative of the Catholic bishops of the United States, makes the official Catholic position clear:

> The financing of schools through public taxation is a responsibility of government, especially of local and state governments. This responsibility entails an obligation to observe the norms of distributive justice in distributing tax funds among the schools within the community. Since government itself has nothing to teach, and because government receives a full return from its educational investment when a school produces well trained citizens, therefore, every school to which parents may send their children in compliance with the compulsory education laws of the State is entitled to a fair share of tax funds. Local and State governments which refuse to support schools not under the control of the local school board are guilty of an injustice against other qualified schools within the community.[1]

The Catholic position was unconstitutional. To be sure, the

19

Supreme Court had never passed on the issue of direct government aid to church schools because it had never been confronted with it. But when it confronted related issues as, for example, in *Everson* v. *Board of Education*, it went out of its way to stress as basic to "no-establishment" of religion that church schools could not be subsidized by government.[2] As we shall see in Chapter 6, while permitting aid for transportation as a safety and welfare measure, the Court shut down hard on any program of direct government aid to the church school. That tight doctrine with the specific language of Everson has been reiterated by the Court in many church-state opinions since.[3]

The no-subsidy-for-church-schools doctrine of the First Amendment which the Supreme Court had so clearly enunciated quickly drew the vocal opposition of the Catholic hierarchy. While the church had won on the issue of transportation in the Everson case, it began to fear that winning that battle might have lost the war. This fear grew with the McCollum decision, which struck down as in violation of the First Amendment, an arrangement in which school children were given sectarian teaching in school rooms during a period of released time.[4] In this case the Court again went out of its way to reassert its tight "money-line" doctrine of the establishment clause. Whereupon the Catholic bishops called upon their people to work peacefully, patiently and perserveringly to supplant the Court's interpretation of the First Amendment with another under which every church institution in the United States could be supported with tax funds.[5]

Here, then, was the problem that confronted John F. Kennedy's drive for the White House in 1960. It was in a way the same problem that had confronted Eisenhower and Truman. It was in a way the same problem that was to confront Johnson. But it was sharpened and dramatized by the fact that Kennedy himself was a Catholic. The Supreme Court had barred government aid to church schools under the First Amendment. The Catholic bishops had publicly repudiated this view and were demanding inclusion of their schools in federal aid to education. Where would Kennedy stand? Here was the nub of the so-called religious issue in the 1960 campaign.

Perhaps the nub lay even deeper than this. Canon Law 1374 of

20

the Roman Catholic Church, theoretically binding on all Catholics, forbade parents to patronize public schools unless the bishop was willing to permit an exception.[6] Since Catholics were thus theoretically forbidden to use the public schools, they could hardly be expected to evidence much enthusiasm or support for them. Where did Kennedy stand on this?

Americans United for Separation of Church and State posed the issue bluntly and then kept the pressure on to see that the candidate had to meet it. This was done in the organization's highly publicized "Questions for a Catholic Candidate," written by Paul Blanshard. Two of the questions are of particular interest here:

> The bishops of your church in an official statement in November, 1948 have denounced the Supreme Court's interpretation of the religion clause of the First Amendment and have urged that the Constitution actually permits the distribution of public money on an equitable basis to sectarian schools and other institutions . . . What is your personal attitude toward your bishops' interpretation of the Constitution, and toward the new plan for financing parochial schools?

> The Canon Law of your church (Canon 1374) directs all American Catholic parents to boycott our public schools unless they receive special permission from their bishops. Do you personally approve or disapprove of this boycott rule?

Amid all the bigot cries Americans United steadily insisted that Senator Kennedy must provide unequivocal answers to these questions. At first, the thing was no big deal to Kennedy. He had probably never heard of Canon 1374 and may have been only vaguely aware of the bishops' feelings. His first reaction was to ignore such matters, reckoning that they might be lost in a general scuffle over the impropriety of raising any religious issue. When he came to understand that this was not going to happen and that forthrightness in this area would be crucial to his campaign, he handled the issue with characteristic firmness. Kennedy formed the habit of answering directly, even bluntly, any question relating to federal aid to church schools. For example, when Fletcher Knebel asked him about it in an interview for *Look* magazine March 3, 1959, he said:

There can be no question of federal funds being used for support of parochial or private schools. It's unconstitutional under the First Amendment as interpreted by the Supreme Court. I'm opposed to the Federal government's extending support to sustain any church or its schools.

Senator Kennedy, making plain the context of his remarks on school aid, then added, "I believe as a senator that the separation of church and state is fundamental to our American concept and heritage and should remain so." And again, "Whatever one's religion in private life may be, for the office holder nothing takes precedence over his oath to uphold the Constitution and all its parts — including the First Amendment and the strict separation of church and state."

It was at Houston that Senator Kennedy won the election. Here, he met head-on the second of the questions Americans United had raised. In a confrontation with the Protestant Ministerial Association of that city, on September 12, 1960, Senator Kennedy cleared away any lingering doubts about his determination to be his own man on the church-state issue. Seldom had a presidential aspirant positioned himself so specifically. The separate Catholic school system was really the heart of the matter, together with the Catholic rule barring the public schools to Catholics. Here is what the Massachusetts Catholic, John F. Kennedy, had to say:

I ask you tonight . . . to judge me on the basis of my declared stand . . . against unconstitutional aid to parochial schools . . . I ask you tonight to judge me on the basis of my declared stand . . . against any boycott of the public schools which I have attended myself.

That did it. That was the clincher on the church-state business. Kennedy had not only opposed federal aid to church schools but also supported the common schools concept. He has specifically stated that he did not feel bound by his church's insistence on separate schools for its constituents. It is said that in politics nothing is fixed. But for the time being, most assuredly, this position was as fixed for Kennedy as anything in politics ever can be. It would have been inconceivable that having made commitments of

22

this kind, and having been elected at least in part as a result, President Kennedy would then have gone before Congress with an aid to education package which included parochial schools. He could not have done so and he did not do so. He made the most comprehensive aid to education proposals that any President had ever made, but he did not include church schools for as much as a nickel. When President Kennedy presented his program to Congress on February 20, 1961, he commented on the church school problem, saying that such schools would be excluded from the bill because to have included them would have been clearly unconstitutional.

Kennedy's position on the religious issue, and especially in the matter of education, was a big factor in his election as President. Put another way, he could not have been elected without such an unequivocal pronouncement. The issue of federal aid to church schools bore far more heavily on him than on his opponent, Vice President Richard M. Nixon. Nixon experienced no particular pressure on the issue. He was, in fact, able to be rather vague on the matter and even to hint on a couple of occasions that something might be done for private schools.

Kennedy was elected. His frank acceptance of the doctrine that the First Amendment effectively barred government aid to church schools delayed such aid for years. It was the forthright nature of the commitment that did it. There was no room for maneuver or compromise. Hence, the anomaly that the first Catholic ever to be elected President set himself adamantly against any federal aid whatever to Catholic schools. Federal aid to elementary and secondary education was a high priority of the Kennedy Administration. It was pressed with vigor. But no general aid bill could be passed during the Kennedy incumbency because the Catholic lobby had sufficient strength to shunt aside any bill which did not provide at least some benefits for Catholic schools.

This was, indeed, virtually the situation that had obtained during the Truman and Eisenhower Administrations. When Rep. Graham Barden, chairman of the House subcommittee on education proposed a bill in 1949 providing federal aid for public schools only, he was publicly attacked by Cardinal Spellman, the unofficial

Roman Catholic primate of the United States. No legislation was passed and the admitted hang-up was the exclusion of the church schools. The Kennedy presence in the White House dramatized and intensified the sectarian issue in federal aid to education. This had the effect of lifting the issue quite out of the milieu of wheeler-dealer politics and entrenching the principals in fixed positions. The Roman Catholic hierarchy was immediately critical of President Kennedy's aid to education proposals. But more than that, the Catholic lobby worked hard to defeat them and eventually succeeded.

The stand of the Catholic hierarchy was set forth by Cardinal Spellman. He was so certain of the way things were to go that he did not even wait for the new President to present his program. On January 17, 1961, the wire services quoted the Cardinal as saying that "it is unthinkable that any American child be denied his share of federal funds because his parents choose for him a God-centered education." In effect, the Cardinal was putting President Kennedy on notice that his aid to education program would have to include the Catholic schools if he expected to get it passed.

There followed one of the most bizarre and fantastic developments in American politics — a grim struggle between the first Catholic President of the United States and the bishops of his own church. Being a political realist, President Kennedy must have understood from the start that he was in for trouble. The Catholic bloc in Congress was strong. Catholics uncritically obedient to their hierarchy were well entrenched in the House Committee on Education and Labor. They took a hard nosed view in support of aid to church schools. There was, moreover, the unfaltering leadership of House Speaker John McCormack who, in sharp disagreement with the President, followed the bishops' line with complete fidelity. This simply meant that there was sufficient strength — though just barely, as it turned out — to bottle up the President's aid to education program in the House.

The Kennedy aid to education bill provoked one of the bitterest legislative struggles in the history of Congress. Things got so tight it was feared the President would yield. The writer had a conference with presidential aide Theodore Sorensen on this issue as the struggle neared its height. Sorensen provided assurance that the President had no intention whatever of altering his position on federal aid to church schools.

There was also a classic meeting between President Kennedy himself and Paul Blanshard, the special counsel of Americans United. Blanshard had become, as a result of his best-seller *American Freedom and Catholic Power,* a prominent critic of the political ambitions of the Roman Catholic Church. As counsel for Americans United, he had prepared the famous "Questions for a Catholic Candidate" which had received so much attention in the 1960 campaign. Kennedy's stirring church-state credo had won Blanshard's support. Blanshard was well aware of the clerical pressures to which Kennedy was being subjected on the school aid issue. He had, indeed, predicted them. Now that the President was caught in the bind, Blanshard was worried. He sought and was granted a personal interview with the President. During this interview Blanshard told Kennedy that as the first Catholic in the White House he must be "pure as Caesar's wife" on the matter of federal aid to church schools. The President laughed and assured Blanshard that he need have no fears on the subject. He intended to put aid to education through, but it would be aid for public schools only — in line with the Constitution and the Supreme Court interpretation of it.

Blanshard asked President Kennedy for a public statement of his position that would reassure the country. The President promised it and it was soon forthcoming. At his press conference on March 1, 1961, the question of federal aid to parochial schools was raised. President Kennedy replied:

> There isn't any room for debate on that subject. It is prohibited by the Constitution and the Supreme Court has made that very clear. Therefore, there would have been no possibility of our recommending it.

The Catholic bishops were not long in replying — one day, to be specific. In a hurriedly convened special session they discussed the matter. There was considerable apprehension about forcing a showdown with the nation's first Catholic President so early in his administration. But in the end Cardinal Spellman's will prevailed and the bishops committed themselves to seek the defeat of any aid to education measures which "discriminated" against their institutions. They said:

> In the event that a federal aid program is enacted which excludes children in private schools, these children will be the victims of discriminatory legislation . . . There will be no alternative but to oppose such discrimination.

In the myriad committee hearings of both bodies, and in the give and take of scores of conferences, the struggle in Congress went on. Again and again, the Catholic leaders made it clear to key legislators that they would defeat the bill if President Kennedy should continue his stubborn insistence that it could include no benefits for their schools. A score of different maneuvers were attempted. As the battle mounted in intensity, President Kennedy asked for a memorandum on the subject of constitutionality of federal aid to church schools. The "Memorandum on the First Amendment to the Constitution Upon Federal Aid to Education" was prepared and issued jointly by the Justice Department and the Department of Health, Education and Welfare on March 28, 1961. Paul Blanshard was a consultant and actually drafted much of the memorandum. It said in part:

> Federal grants to sectarian schools for general educational purposes would run squarely into the prohibitions of the First Amendment as interpreted in the *Everson, McCollum* and *Zorach* cases. Grants of assistance in the construction of general school facilities and for increasing teachers' salaries . . . are the clear case of what is proscribed by the Constitution. . . . Aid by way of grants to sectarian schools could only be justified by a reversal of the Supreme Court's interpretation of the establishment clause and a new interpretation which would regard it as merely prohibiting discrimination among religions.

The big issue eventually came to hang upon a much smaller issue as often happens in such matters. Catholic Action sought to impose a lien on the President's education bill in the form of an amendment providing for long term "soft" loans for parochial school construction. Then it became a question whether this would be in the form of a rider on the main education bill, or whether it would be handled as a separate item. Rep. James J. Delaney of New York, an intimate of Cardinal Spellman, was the swing man on the House Rules Committee where the fate of the bill was finally settled. Delaney argued that as a separate item the Catholic measure would have no chance, but that if it were attached to the main bill it would be swallowed as a necessary compromise to get an aid bill passed. When the House Rules Committee voted to keep the matters separate, Delaney swung his vote against the President's bill and it was denied a "rule" to come to the floor, by an 8 to 7 margin. House Speaker John McCormack was privy to all this backstage maneuvering. Had the bill reached the floor it would have passed easily. As it was, Delaney's vote killed it.

In a subsequent interview with the Washington *Evening Star*, January 22, 1965, Rep. Delaney explained his stand this way:

Q. Is it fair to say you killed Kennedy's school bill?

A. Yes, the bill was discriminatory. . . . It would have helped only public schools.

Q. Does the Johnson bill, in general, meet your objections to the Kennedy bill?

A. Yes. It makes the child, not the school, the beneficiary of the program.

The assassin's bullets which struck down President Kennedy in November, 1963, had a great many side effects. One of the most curious was that of making possible a program of federal school aid which would include benefits for church schools. It is possible that a second term for President Kennedy might have brought an easement to this impasse. If he had been reelected in a sweep with a large Democratic majority, he might then have been in position to wheel and deal on the issue of aid to religious schools. Or he might have been strong enough to bull through an aid bill for public schools only.

The Kennedy experience with aid to education provides the background necessary to understand the situation Johnson faced when Congress convened early in 1965. Johnson had promised what Kennedy had tried hard for but failed to deliver. If he were to make good, he felt he must come up with a formula that would satisfy the Catholic leaders without alienating either the Protestants or the public school people. A formula must be found to avoid the impasse that stopped Kennedy. Aid must be provided for Catholic schools — not directly, of course, for the Supreme Court had been clear on that. But was there not some indirect way, an end run?

Johnson had won decisively in the 1964 election. The political strength he possessed as he commenced his new term in 1965 was overwhelming. A popular mandate of the dimensions achieved by Johnson in the 1964 election conveys pervasive power. His election sweep was reenforced by overwhelming Democratic majorities in both Houses of Congress. In the wake of such a victory, before fissures have time to develop, a triumphant President can get from Congress almost anything he wants. In early 1965, Johnson was in position to get the long delayed federal aid to education. There can be no question about this: an aid program for public schools only could have passed the Congress without any concession whatever to the Catholic leadership. After all, Kennedy had just missed it by a whisker, though he was in a much weaker position. His bill — for public schools only — had passed the Senate in a breeze and would have done quite as well in the House save for that unfortunate 8 to 7 adverse vote in the Rules Committee which kept it from coming to the floor. Now Johnson had the political logistics to put it through. The obstructionist tactics of the clerics might have been a nuisance, but nothing more. Had Johnson followed the Kennedy line and buckled down to work, he could have done it.

The fact is, however, that the President compromised with the Catholic Church. When he and his Administration got down to the business of devising the aid formula, they found themselves up against the old church-state barrier. The Johnson team discovered that the church-state matter was not just one problem among many. It was *the problem*. The determination of the Catholic lobbyists cannot be discounted. Ninety percent of the private schools in the United States are sectarian and about 93 percent of these are operated by the Roman Catholic Church. These churchmen realized that if a federal aid formula were established which did not include their institutions they might never be included.

28

Opposed to their ambitions in the states were constitutional provisions so strict and specific that basic amendments seemed to offer the only hope. On the federal scene there was also a discouraging barrier — the First Amendment and the tight construction which the Supreme Court had given it. But the First Amendment language was more vague and seemed to offer room for maneuver.

During the campaign of 1964, and even as Congress convened, Johnson never dealt directly with the issue of government aid to sectarian schools as Kennedy had done. He never discussed the matter openly and frankly, but talked vaguely of aiding all children. He promised to avoid the old church-state hang-up without ever indicating how he would do it. He never dealt in specifics with this question, offering, instead, just enough vague generality to give some comfort to everybody. Kennedy had been completely candid; Johnson was considerably less than candid. When Johnson finally came forward with his aid to education proposals, they offered major concessions to the Catholic Church. In doing so, they struck a heavy glow at separation of church and state. Yet even as the bill was introduced, it was accompanied by a continuing campaign of deception which sought to conceal its real nature from the American people.

Formidable as the Catholic lobby was, Johnson was more formidable still. Why, then, did he seek a compromise with this church? The answer may lie in the nature of the President himself. His passion to be liked and approved has been widely recognized. Perhaps he could not stand the thought of putting through an aid to education bill that did not delight everyone. Perhaps he felt the need of political support in a sector where John F. Kennedy did not have to worry at all.

Much of the credit for Johnson's compromise on the school aid bill belongs to the Catholic lobbyists headed by Msgr. Frederick G. Hochwalt of the United States Catholic Conference. He and his co-workers knew that it was now or never for their church. They put on one of the most intensive and astute legislative efforts ever seen in Congress. Perhaps the most amazing thing about it was that so little of it got in the press. The public simply did not know what was going on.

29

The Catholic leaders understood the situation perfectly. They knew that they must not let aid to education pass without tying the parochial schools into it in some way. The public schools only kind of federal aid must never be permitted to get in motion. If that happened, they could forget about government aid for another generation. But if they succeeded, if they got even so much as a foot in the door, they could go on from there. The beginning was the only time and the ground floor was the only place for them. The battle in 1961 had been savage. The one in 1965 was tougher still. Every kind of political persuasion known to man was vigorously applied. The maneuvers within the committee were fantastic. House Speaker John McCormack threw the full weight of his office on the side of aiding the parochial schools. Finally, the Catholic lobbyists won. The word was passed down that a way must be found to put the Catholic schools in the bill.

Nothing better indicates the political astuteness of Lyndon B. Johnson and his administration than the manner in which they went about the business of arranging the fatal concession on the church-state issue and then selling it to the public. Once the decision had been made to compromise with the Catholic Church, every possible stratagem was employed to do the job smoothly and expeditiously. First of all, the Johnson leaders turned to the churchmen. In this particular snow job they were almost completely successful. They eventually succeeded in building a formidable churchmen's consensus in favor of a bill which included solid benefits for parochial schools. When one considers that virtually all the major Protestant denominations had repeatedly positioned themselves against that very thing, this feat becomes all the more impressive. The Johnson team realized that the particular formula for church school aid was less important than the feelings of the churchmen. If their bill proved unacceptable and they were to have these people on their back, no plan could hope to succeed. The country would be immersed in inter-creedal hostilities that could frustrate any program even if passed into law. It was the religious leaders who must be mollified and persuaded and it was to the religious leaders that they turned.

First, the Roman Catholic leadership must be satisfied. As the

30

legislation, later to be known as the Elementary and Secondary Education Act of 1965, was being drafted, Msgr. Frederick G. Hochwalt, the top Catholic education lobbyist, was in and out of congressional offices daily. He sat in on long sessions with committee members making clear to them what would and would not be acceptable to his church. The church school compromise which eventually emerged was in substantial detail devised by Msgr. Hochwalt and approved by him. It was a small package as federal spending goes these days, but it was a beginning. The church schools were in. Some in the Catholic community began to complain that they were not getting enough, but their leaders hushed them at once! At that point, only the beginning mattered, only the precedent.

Bringing the Protestant leadership into the grand consensus was scarcely less important. The problem here was to get the Protestants to accept the concessions which the bill had made to the Catholics. The brunt of the effort was carried by two prominent Baptist leaders in the administration — Brooks Hays and Bill Moyers. Hays, a former congressman, had served as president of the mammoth Southern Baptist Convention. He was a kind of religious troubleshooter for the Johnson Administration. Moyers, also a prominent Baptist, was for a considerable period President Johnson's right-hand man. Their biggest assignment on the education bill was to get the Baptists in line. Hays and Moyers began their effort with Dr. C. Emanuel Carlson, executive director of the Baptist Joint Committee on Public Affairs. They were completely successful with Dr. Carlson, convincing him that the legislation in the form proposed would not trespass upon separation of church and state. Carlson joined the consensus and used his influence to place Presidential aide Bill Moyers before the Southern Baptist Convention in Dallas, Texas, just at the time the aid bill was working its way through Congress. Moyers reassured the dubious Southern Baptists that while the legislation was designed to aid the education of all children it contained nothing contrary to their Baptist traditions. Carlson himself came out for the bill, stating that "most of the church-state issues in President Johnson's education bill have been eliminated."[7]

31

Dr. Arthur S. Flemming, then vice president, later president, of the National Council of Churches, was an early convert. When President Johnson's proposals in the form of the Elementary and Secondary Education Act were before Congress, Flemming offered favorable testimony as the Council's spokesman. He praised the legislation as basically sound. Much of the leg work was done by the Rev. Dean M. Kelley, head of the Council's Religious Liberty Department. Kelley was soon convinced that the formula devised by the Subcommittee on Education was one that could resolve the church-state problem which had stymied federal aid to education for so long. Kelley even claimed to have originated the church school formula in the Elementary and Secondary Education Act. He undertook to convince the unofficial church-state consortium of Protestant leaders in Washington that the formula did not trespass upon church-state separation. He was the catalyst through whom the Administration quietly undertook to assemble a grand consensus of religious leaders favorable to the bill. Exulted Kelley: "Main Protestant bodies of the nation have found a common ground with Roman Catholics on which they can accept the President's proposal for federal aid to educationally deprived children."[8]

The third member (with Carlson and Kelley) of the Administration's church-state trio was Dr. H.B. Sissel, secretary for National Affairs for the United Presbyterian Church, U.S.A. Sissel was later to lose his job because his thinking on ESEA did not accurately reflect that of his denomination. But he was the man on the scene at the time and his enthusiastic endorsement of the bill carried considerable weight. He purported to represent the Presbyterians. Dr. Sissel praised the committee for producing a bill which "seeks to avoid placing the Congress . . . again on the horns of the old church-state dilemma. . . ."[9]

These were the men who joined President Johnson's grand consensus. They took care of the Protestant community and by sitting heavily on the lid saw to it that it did not pop off in a nasty religious controversy. There can be no doubt that the support given by these men in the name of the National Council of Churches, the Baptists and the Presbyterians was a decisive factor in the passage of ESEA. In retrospect, it must appear that these men were politically naive or that they simply did not care about separation of church and state and knowingly helped pass legislation which seriously undermined it.

There were at least four groups, however, that were not engulfed by the consensus. They were Americans United for Separation of Church and State, the National Association of Evangelicals, the American Civil Liberties Union and the Jewish community. All perceived that the Johnson formula was no more than a device to circumvent the stricture of the First Amendment regarding acts respecting establishment of religion.

Glenn L. Archer, executive director of Americans United, warned repeatedly of the administrative latitude which the loosely drawn legislation would permit. He called attention to an old political cliche that where administrative discretion is involved one can always assume the worst. The writer appeared at all the committee hearings, carefully dissecting the bills, showing how their effect would be to subvert the First Amendment by providing government subsidies to church institutions.[10] A favorite device was to recall the Kennedy memorandum from the Department of Health, Education and Welfare which made clear that the First Amendment barred federal aid to church schools. The writer quoted it copiously at every opportunity, much to the solons' embarrassment. Yet the Democratic leaders went right on with the business of repudiating the late President's position and his legal advisors as well.

The Jewish groups, particularly the American Jewish Congress, were not fooled for a moment. The National Association of Evangelicals was the only major Protestant group that held out from the consensus. The NAE represented a group of smaller, conservative denominations. It was not as politically prestigious as the liberal denominations which formed the National Council of Churches. Its warnings were not heeded.

Many looked to the National Education Association to provide decisive opposition to the Catholic compromise in the Elementary and Secondary Education Act of 1965. They were completely disappointed, for the NEA agreed to sharing the funds with parochial schools as a necessary compromise to get the bill passed. Five years

33

later NEA dramatically reversed its position, but it was too late. The damage was done.

What strategy did the Johnson Administration devise to circumvent the Constitution and the Supreme Court? With what magic formula did its leaders succeed in allaying the fears of the religious leaders and fashioning a strong consensus capable of passing federal aid legislation which included parochial schools? The Catholic leaders themselves had to marvel at it. They have described the Elementary and Secondary Education Act of 1965 as "a tribute to the 89th Congress and to its ingenuity in circumventing antediluvian preconceptions."[11] The reference was, of course, to the separation of church and state. Before describing the formula, let us rehearse the situation which President Johnson faced. Congress was specifically forbidden by the First Amendment to make any law respecting an establishment of religion. The Supreme Court had applied the ban to tax support of church schools. In the face of this prohibition, the administration's leaders undertook to make a law which would provide government financing for the educational institutions of the church. Obviously, they could not meet the problem head on; they had to work an end run.

The Supreme Court, for all its adamant insistence that church schools could not be subsidized by government, had perhaps unwittingly given the Johnson leaders an opening. In the *Everson* case the Court had suggested a line of thinking which did not escape protagonists of federal aid to church schools. In that case the Court approved transportation assistance to children in Catholic schools on the ground that this was not an educational matter, not even incidentally aid to a religious school, but purely a welfare benefit to the child himself. The architects of church school aid saw an opening here. Why could not other forms of aid be devised for church schools that could be described as benefits to the child? Their constitutionality could be pleaded on the ground that they did not assist the school, only the welfare of the child in it.

So originated the child benefit theory. While it did not really have its origin in *Everson*, it was, in a sense, triggered by *Everson*.

34

The promoters of the Elementary and Secondary Education Act stressed this theory. They said that what they sought was to help children — all children — get a good education. And to this they quickly added another selling point. The legislation was not only to help children, it was to help *poor* children. The strength of this posture was formidable. Opponents were put in the position of fighting against children, and poor children at that!

The use of the poverty gimmick was indicated even before the election in a UPI story which appeared widely in the press January 22, 1964. The story referred to the church-state controversy with which President Kennedy had been forced to contend and said that President Johnson would be able to avoid this by including aid to parochial schools in an attack on poverty. The story brought out that:

> Roman Catholic educators have been privately consulted about the Johnson proposals and are prepared to support them on the understanding that parochial schools will participate. . . . In an effort to minimize controversy over the church-state issue, the administration will emphasize that its program is not designed to aid schools, public or private, but rather seeks to use schools to help poor children break out of the "circle of poverty."

Poverty thus became a useful slogan especially when coupled with child benefit. Champions of government subsidy to church schools were enabled to present themselves as the saviors of poor children. The trouble with the child benefit theory, however, was that it was too good. You could use it to justify government aid to virtually every kind of church program. Anything done for a school would, presumably, benefit the children in it and vice versa. Though the bill provided only incidentally for church school construction, a much fuller program of this nature could be defended on the ground, for example, that a nice building would benefit the children who were thus sheltered and warmed. As for aiding religion, what is religious about brick and mortar? There is, in fact, no form of aid to church schools that cannot be rationalized by the child benefit theory. Yet the appeal of child benefit to the welfare instincts of the country found ready response.

The Johnson Administration used yet another device — that of assistance in special categories, above and beyond the regular curriculum. Here the argument ran that of course it would be unconstitutional to provide for the regular work-a-day schooling in the parochial institutions, but extras could be provided. For example, it would be unconstitutional to pay with federal funds for a reading course in a church school, but it would be constitutional to pay for a remedial reading course. One day a long argument broke out among committee members as to the difference between reading and remedial reading!

The Johnson formula was explained by Rep. Frank Thompson (D-N.Y.) in language intended to provide a guiding legislative history for the act:

> Services and arrangements provided for nonpublic school students in nonpublic schools must be special as distinguished from general educational assistance. The decision about the best arrangement for providing special educational assistance under Title I is left to the public education agency of the school district, under the Constitution and laws of the State. Thus, public school boards could make available the services of such special personnel as guidance counsellors, speech therapists, remedial reading specialists, school social workers who would reach the nonpublic school children in the public schools, or through public services in the nonpublic buildings, or through mobile services, or through ETV, or through community centers, etc. [12]

This might have seemed sufficiently vague to satisfy everyone, but not so. The battle was, in fact, only beginning. For once the bill had been signed into law, the mischief of "administrative discretion" promptly showed up. It is the administrative procedures designed by the administrators themselves which actually determine how the programs will be handled, and, to get to the nitty-gritty, who will get what. The Protestant leaders who had sold the consensus to their constituents were amazed to discover that when the administrative regulations were promulgated they contained none of the elaborate reassurances by which they had been induced to accept the bill! Most of the careful fictions that had been created to blunt the impression of direct church school aid had simply disappeared at the insistence of the United States Catholic Conference. Meetings were held with the disgruntled Protestant leaders and Office of Education leaders who were implementing the church school aid programs. There was little or no concession to the Protestants. Dr. Carlson remarked bitterly that unless something was done on the church-state situation he would have to confess to his constituents that he had been wrong in his appraisal of the legislation.[13] The Baptist leader even told friends he was giving serious thought to submitting his resignation. Dean Kelley ws equally perturbed.

The indignation of the Protestant leadership was understandable. They realized that they had been taken. For amid the studied ambiguities of ESEA, grants were unquestionably flowing into church schools in a manner they had not contemplated. How could this have happened? On the face, the law was not unconstitutional. It did not mention parochial schools. It even contains the following solemn disclaimer:

Nothing contained in the Act shall be construed to authorize the making of any payment under this Act, or under any Act amended by this Act, for religious worship or instruction.

Yet ESEA has managed under all of its titles to provide important financial aid for schools which are basic operations of churches. The law speaks of educational aid to children enrolled in private schools. Title I provides "special educational services and arrangements (such as dual enrollment), educational radio and television, and mobile educational services and equipment." Title II provides for "library resources, textbooks and other instructional materials" for students in private schools. Title III provides that supplementary activities and services provided under the program" are to be made available to students in private schools.

The casual reader of this legislation might envisage nothing but a plethora of private, secular schools participating in the federal programs. But, as we have previously pointed out, 90 percent of the private schools involved are sectarian, and of these about 93 percent are owned by one church.

The clincher on the true intent of the legislation is to be seen in the determinaton to override state constitutional barriers against government aid to church schools. Ordinarily, the administrative agent for the federal program is the state board of education. But as soon as the program got underway it became evident to all, as it had previously been to many, that numerous state administrators would be estopped by their own constitutional provisions from administering the aid provided for church schools. The Johnson consensus had carefully prepared for that eventuality, however. Its leaders had inserted a stipulation that if state officials were forbidden by specific provisions in their own constitutions from transmitting Title II aid to private schools, then federal officials would step in and do it anyway.

The eroding effect on the church-state arrangements in the states was immediate. There was pressure on the states to make their own provisions and practices to conform with those of the Federal Government. This was true not only of the pressure exerted on their administrative apparatus. It had legislative effects as well. The situation in New York State provides an instance. In 1965, the New York Legislature passed a bill providing textbooks for students in parochial schools. Governor Rockefeller asked the attorney general for a ruling as to its constitutionality since it appeared that on its face it violated the New York Constitution. The attorney general promptly gave his opinion that the bill was unconstitutional. Despite this, Gov. Rockefeller signed the bill into law. He did so on the theory that since the Federal Government was providing textbooks for church school students, New York ought to be able to do it, too. Indeed, constitutionality of the law was eventually upheld by the courts.

A good example of this conflict can be seen in the case of shared time or dual enrollment arrangements under Title I. Some of the bill's sponsors had touted this as the principal means of aid to church schools, while many church educators have thought of it as a means of buttressing church schools which are too poor to maintain an adequate program of their own. Some state courts — e.g., the Missouri Supreme Court — and attorneys general of a number of other states, have held the practice to be contrary to

38

state constitutions or statutory provisions.

The attitude of the Catholic leadership toward the church-state restrictions in the states is illustrated by the Boston College study which urged that any states with constitutional problems of this kind should have their aid funds cut until they could get rid of the offending provisions.[14]

Within two years of its passage ESEA had delivered such a wallop to state provisions for separation of church and state that this writer advised a Congressional committee:

> We have come face to face with the question as to whether the states are to be permitted any policy-making role at all, or whether they are to be altogether subsumed by the federal power. Are the states to be permitted in their laws a tight, strict concept of separation of church and state? Or, will the federal power simply override and beat down this concept by the sheer weight of its money power, forcing on the states programs and procedures which are specifically forbidden by their laws? To put it another way, shall the states which desire to establish and sustain a single system of public schools serving the entire community have forced on them, instead, the business of planning for and supporting various systems of religious schools as well?

ESEA itself was being regularly subjected to sectarian abuse. As its opponents had predicted, once the administrators went to work the various programs shed their safeguards and became direct subsidies to church schools. Indeed, where church political power was predominent, sectarian leaders were able to manipulate the programs to their own advantage and claim the lion's share of the funds. A study of ESEA in the schools of New York City disclosed that sectarian interests in that area preempted the programs and operated them in a manner which showed gross favoritism to the children attending sectarian schools and discrimination against those attending public schools.[15]

In practice, the various church-state restrictions envisaged by the naive academicians were simply ignored. For example, Title I instruction for church school students was typically offered in church schools rather than in public schools or in neutral buildings. Services were provided for whole schools or classes rather than to individual students.

As for the library aid offered under Title II, the church-state safeguards that were envisaged simply vanished in the practical operations. This is the way it works. After receiving his allotment figure, the church school administrator submits his order based on the assumption that, once it is filled, these items will remain permanently in the church school library. The order is sent in. It is presumably checked to see if the books requested are really of a secular nature and compatible with the standards of the state. (How much checking there may be at this point is problematical.) Then the order is forwarded, with payment, to the publisher. The books are sent to the church school bearing the stamp "public property" and an inventory of these items is to be placed in the files of the appropriate public authority. Within a few years the church school will have accumulated many shelves filled with publicly owned books on permanent loan. To all practical intent these books then belong to the school itself. This is a church school subsidy, pure and simple.

In his survey of 60 school districts in New Jersey made during the 1966-67 school year, George LaNoue found an almost total disregard of church-state restrictions and safeguards in the administration of ESEA aid to church schools.[16] LaNoue found that 58 percent of the parochial students receiving Title I instructional services and 40 percent of those receiving supplementary services were aided right in the parochial schools. He found that dual enrollment programs were few in number. He observed that "once a project goes into a parochial school it is generally impossible to avoid aiding the school or to exercise meaningful public control over the public personnel and equipment." LaNoue also discovered that despite House Report No. 1814 which stated that no public agency was to assign personnel to private schools on a full time basis, exactly this was being done in sixty-six percent of the cases.

LaNoue found an almost studied carelessness in regard to church-state matters in the administration of ESEA. There was a quick espousal of simplistic solutions. There was also a disposition to regard federal funds as a kind of bonus that one did not need to be too fussy about. Finally, since local public school officials were legally responsible for administration of aid programs, this meant that they were the persons who had to grapple with these problems. The pressures were many and such officials exhibited an understandable timidity about avoiding any additional ones.

Spot checks on the operations of ESEA indicate that in regard to educational equipment and materials, these are for all practical purposes given outright to the church schools. As had been anticipated by critics, once the business of assigning publicly paid teachers to church schools commenced, there was little control over what they were to teach. The concept of special courses tended to break down as the teachers were assigned to general duties in the school. Remedial reading tended to become reading and special mathematics to become mathematics.

Most conspicuous of all, perhaps, is the failure of the poverty concept in the administering of ESEA funds to church schools. The elaborate formula for allocation on the basis of the number of disadvantaged children in a given district is difficult to apply for public school children and even more difficult for parochial school children. No data are available in most cases. The parochial schools have as a rule a much lower percentage of disadvantaged children than the public schools, which further complicates matters. What harassed administrators do, therefore, is exactly what might have been anticipated. They tend to lop off a share for the parochials based on a straight percentage of the total students they educate.

Occasionally, public authorities agree to assume financing of an entire church school. They do this on the pretext that the school in question is a poverty school or an experimental school which makes it something out of the ordinary and therefore justifies federal financing. In Louisville, Ky., the Roman Catholic Church had been closing up its inner city schools because of budgetary problems. Its leaders turned to the Federal Government for financial aid. They did this by seeking a Title IV grant via Ursuline College, a church institution in Louisville.

Thus, three of the inner city schools were merged under a single group of church administrators. This, and the practice of not grading the students, are said to make the school an experimental institution, different from a regular school. Another experimental feature would be the supervision of Ursuline College through which the federal funds to support the school would be channeled. Other special features of the school are said to be a nursery-kindergarten program, after school and summer projects, and field trips. There is nothing experimental or out of the ordinary about these features, most of which would be normal to any school. This is simply a program by which the Catholic Church keeps alive three of its schools taught by religious clad in their clerical garb. They are doing it with government money channeled through one church institution into another under the guise of something innovative.

An exhaustive report on the operations of Title I has been made by the Southern Center for Studies in Public Policy and the NAACP Legal Defense and Education Fund. It sheds further light on the failure of the poverty concept in federal aid. After a comprehensive nationwide survey, these groups state that: "Our hopes that the Nation would finally begin to rectify the injustices and inequities which poor children suffer from being deprived of an equal educational opportunity have been sorely disappointed."[17] The reason for this is quickly discerned. Whatever the particular form of aid, it is simply directed to the general improvement of the school, whether public or private. Indeed, the federal funds are often used to finance existing school programs and services. The survey charges that the formula which calls for aid in terms of the number of disadvantaged children is not employed in most instances.

The study points out, incidentally, that sometimes the church-state violations become flagrant. In Detroit, Title I funds were used to purchase Temple Baptist Church at a cost of $1.4 million. This property was supposed to house the administrative headquarters for Title I projects. But it was discovered that only a small portion of the building was ever used for this purpose. HEW auditors concluded that "the greatest benefactor to date appears to have been the Temple Baptist Church congregation which continued to use the building about as before."[18]

A good illustration of how Title II works in actual practice may be seen in the case of Cardinal Newman High School of Santa Rosa, Calif. This school has had its library completely stocked and furnished by the Federal Government. How could this be in a country which constitutionally separates church and state and government has been forbidden to finance church schools? The prospectus of the school in which it applied for the grant is revealing. It tells of the desire of this school to provide a library which would be a "living laboratory" for students and teachers. The prospectus states that the school's plan calls for a "model, multi-media library." The school, it is said, sought to demonstrate what could be done in the way of a quality library at a small, secondary school.

After the bright depiction of what they sought to accomplish, the applicants noted that, alas, there was one major drawback: they had no funds to achieve it. Their only hope for the attainment of this rare and extra-special library was through Title II of ESEA. How this library differed from any other library, it is difficult to see. In fact, it did not differ from others. Despite the fancy names and all the high flown verbiage, it was just a school library and they wanted to get government money to pay for it. Reading the prospectus one is made to realize that the applicants are striving hard for effect. They seek to present their school library as something out of the ordinary and extra-special in order to provide justification for ESEA financing of the project. But what emerges is the spectacle of a church school being financed in part with federal funds. For the project was approved with an initial grant of $32,400 for materials and there will undoubtedly be a continuing government obligation to this institution.

Although Title III contained elaborate safeguards against sectarian abuse, this part of the law, too, has been used to finance programs for church schools.

Still another example of the government aid to specials which benefit church schools is that provided under the Cooperative Research Act which has channeled funds to these institutions for various types of programs. For example, in 1970, the Los Angeles Catholic archdiocese received $40,000 to put on a right-to-read summer program for both parochial and public school children. The announced purpose of the grant is to show that parochial school teachers can help attack the reading problems of disadvantaged children. The teaching will be done in parochial school rooms by nuns of the Catholic Church clad in their clerical garb.

After six years of ESEA it is clear that the Federal Government is steadily channeling funds into church schools. As a result of this Act which has received good funding and which has since been broadened and enlarged, and as a result of parallel legislation now being developed in the states, many predict that church schools are destined to receive their basic budgets from government. The ruses and subterfuges by which the church lobbyists are accomplishing this result have been described. What needs to be stated is that this procedure does change the entire church-state picture in the United States. These funds feed the structure of the church just as surely as if they were paid directly to the clergy.

The integral relationship of a church school to a church is quickly established. The largest system of church schools by far in the United States is that of the Roman Catholic Church. By definition of its highest authorities, this system exists for the purposes of the church. It exists for the purpose of giving Catholic students a Catholic-oriented education in which all subjects are to be permeated with Catholic doctrine. Pope Pius XI said in his *Christian Education of Youth,* 1929, that the only school which his church could approve was one in which "the Catholic religion permeates the entire atmosphere (and where) the whole organization of the school and its teachers, syllabus and textbooks in every branch is regulated by the Christian (i.e. Catholic) spirit." Every Pope since has consistently adhered to this view as have the pronouncements of Vatican II. The logic of Justice Jackson's dissent in *Everson* appears inexorable:

> I should be very surprised if any Catholic would deny that the parochial school is a vital, if not the most vital part of the Roman Catholic Church. If put to the choice, that venerable institution, I should expect, would forego its whole service for mature persons before it would give up education of the young, and it would be a wise choice. Its growth and cohesion, discipline and loyalty, spring from its schools. Catholic

44

education is the rock on which the whole structure rests, and to render tax aid to its church school is indistinguishable to me from rendering the same aid to the church itself.[19]

The Catholic parish school is physically owned, as is the church, by the diocesan bishop. The priest who runs the parish and its school is appointed to his dual post by the bishop who, in turn, is appointed by the Pope. In a comprehesive survey of Catholic education, edited by James Michael Lee who heads the Department of Education at Notre Dame, it was found that Catholic schools were typically dominated by clerics.[20] A majority of parish schools even now have no board of laymen. Where such boards exist they have little or no authority. The typical parish publishes no audited financial reports; nor does the diocese. The schools which are 98 percent Catholic in enrollment require religious studies and observances of the students and recruit for religious professions among them. The school is the church; the church is the school. Justice Jackson declared that to subsidize the one is to subsidize the other.

We have presented a considerable delineation of the religious nature of the Catholic school. The same thing could be done with equal clarity for other denominational schools. Whether the school be Lutheran, Seventh-day Adventist, Christian Reformed, Christian Day, or whatever the denomination, the religious thrust is apparent. Indeed, why else would churches have schools? The religious motivation of the church school glows in this statement by Arthur W. Owens, spokesman for Powderhorn Park (Minneapolis) Christian School: "There is a completely different attitude at Powderhorn and other Christian oriented schools. God and the Bible are tied into everything."[21]

One can take any one of these programs of government aid to church schools, in isolation, and work out a legal rationale for it which sounds good. Exactly this is being done, and there is a chance it may be successful in deluding the public and even the courts. But if we look at the entire picture in composite, these elaborate rationales appear absurd. The sheer dimensions of the aid and its extension to the most sensitive areas of clerical need, point inexorably to religious establishment. It is coming by the back door, but it is coming. The tax for religion looms. Its burden is steadily increasing and there seems to be no end of it in sight. The only development that can save the people from this new/old form of oppression is abrupt revulsion of public opinion. There is some evidence that this is about to occur.

President Nixon announced on March 3, 1970 creation of a Commission on School Finance of which Neil H. McElroy was chairman and Norman Karsh executive director. There were sixteen members, educators selected from the ranks of schoolmen, both public and private. President Nixon's own expressions of interest in providing federal aid for Catholic schools seemed to set a tone of parochial expectation for the Commission's work. This impression was further enhanced by the appointment of a special private and parochial panel to serve as a part of the larger commission. This group not only participated and voted as part of the Commission, but also was empowered to make recommendations of its own. On the panel were such diehard parochial advocates as Bishop William E. McManus, head of Chicago's Catholic Schools, Clarence Walton, president of Catholic University of America, Ivan L. Zylstra and William Saltonstall. All but Saltonstall were known champions of public subsidies to church schools, and he had been for years headmaster of a private school. This group constituted from the start a solid bloc of pro-parochi-aiders on the Commission.

Even so, the Commission which reported on March 6, 1972 barely came through with its foreordained recommendations. The Commission divided right down the middle. The recommendations favoring various forms of federal aid to private schools eventually passed by two votes with a strong minority, including Chairman Neil McElroy, in opposition. Favored in the squeaker vote were such forms of additional aid to parochial schools as tax credits, tuition grants, scholarships and "equitable sharing in any new federally supported assistance programs." Chairman McElroy and seven members of the Commission objected, saying that such recommendations would only raise hopes which could not be fulfilled. Said the chairman:

46

With all the ingenuity that has been tried, and certainly it has been tried in New York State and tried by a large number of dedicated individuals who are concerned deeply with non-public schools, it really has been impossible to find any proposal that looks as if it would withstand the two tests of feasibility and judicial acceptance.

The President's Commission on School Finance probably reflects national sentiment on the parochiaid issue with some accuracy. There is a cadre of support centering in the professional churchmen whose institutions are steadily declining. This cadre is able to exert considerable political pressure since it lifts before politicians the threat of a shiftable bloc vote. Most elections are close. If government aid is an issue that can swing even a small bloc of votes from one column to the other, then respectful consideration must be given to it. Parochiaid advocates buttress their case by holding up the specter of a large group of parents anxious to send their children to parochial schools if only the government would put up the money.

Anti-parochiaid leaders envisage another bloc, however, It includes Catholic parents who reject their church's historic insistence on sectarian segregation in education. These parents are now patronizing the public schools and they want these schools to be good schools. It includes many others who insist on excellent public schools and resent diversion of their funds among a plethora of private schools. The politician who has traditionally thought in terms of a Catholic bloc to be attracted to his column by his espousal of parochiaid may now have begun to rethink his strategy. There may be a developing bloc on the opposite side of this issue.

Notes

1. Hearings, Senate Subcommittee on Education, 1947, pp.310-11

2. 330 U.S. 1; 333 U.S. 201 (1947)

3. *McCollum v. Board of Education.* 333 U.S. 203 (1948)
   Zorach v. Clauson. 343 U.S. 306 (1952)

Torcaso v. Watkins. 367 U.S. 488 (1961)

Abington School District v. Schempp. 374 U.S. 488 (1963)

4. Op. Cit.

5. *The Christian in Action.* Statement of the Bishops of the United States. Nov. 21, 1948

6. *Canon Law, a Text and Commentary.* Third Revised Edition, by T. Lincoln Bouscaren and Adam C. Ellis, Bruce Publishing Co., Milwaukee. p. 744

7. *Baptist Public Affairs News Service.* Feb. 9, 1965

8. Brooklyn *Tablet.* Feb. 25, 1965

9. Subcommittee on Education Hearings S. 370, Part 5, p.370

10. *Federal Aid to Parochial Schools.* Testimony presented to Congressional Committees, Americans United, Silver Spring, Md.

11. Nuccio, Vincent C. and Walsh, John J., *Toward a Partnership in Education. Government and Private Schools* (no pagination)

12. *Congressional Record.* 1965, p.5572

13. An interesting account of these events can be found in Richard E. Morgan's *The Politics of Religious Conflict.* Pegasus, N.Y., pp.91ff

14. Nuccio and Walsh, op. cit.

15. *The Church State Problem - a Guide for Community Groups.* American Civil Liberties Union

16. *Rutgers Law Review.* Winter 1968, Vol. 22, No. 2

17. *Title I of ESEA - Is It Helping Poor Children?.* Washington, D.C. p.1

18. Ibid. p.46

19. 330 U.S. 1, 333 U.S. 201 (1947)

20. Lee, James Michael. *Catholic Education in the Western World.* U. of Notre Dame Press, 1967, p.272

21. *Religious News Service.* May 13, 1970

4.   The Church-State Battle
in the States

Following their initial success with the federal aid to education proposals, advocates of government aid to church schools have turned their attention to the states. Though their task is far more difficult at this level, they employ the same tactics of circumvention. They seek to obtain by ruse and deception the state aid for their institutions which may not be given directly. In this endeavor they use the federal programs as a club to bludgeon the states into line. These tactics are producing results. We now see in the states the beginnings of the same kind of church-state involvements which already characterize the national scene.

We have noted that the church-state provisions in the various state constitutions are much tighter than the religion clause of the First Amendment. The reason for this is that the state provisions for the most part came later and by the time they came there had been serious controversies over just what the First Amendment meant. The first part of the First Amendment merely stated that "Congress shall make no law respecting an establishment of religion or prohibiting the free exercise thereof." Even in the early days following approval of this amendment there was some difference of opinion as to its meaning. Did it mean, for example, that public funds could not be used for the support of churches on a nondiscriminatory basis? State establishments of religion persisted until 1833, since only a national establishment of religion was originally barred by the First Amendment. (The Fourteenth

Amendment which extended federal proscriptions to the states was not passed until after the Civil War.)

Besides this, the whole matter of tax support of education became an issue subsequent to the First Amendment. Following long experiments with denominational schools, a public school system began to develop — a free, open system supported by taxation and nonsectarian in nature. Should the sectarian schools which persisted receive a share of the tax support, or not?

The legislative history of the First Amendment makes it amply clear that its authors intended to include a ban on government financing of religion. How better to establish a religion than to finance it? But religious leaders are never easily convinced on such a matter. If the founding fathers had meant for the First Amendment to bar the tax for religion, why had they not specifically said so? And, if they did mean to bar taxes for church support, did this ban apply also to the schools of churches?

The drafters of the state constitutions proposed to erase any lingering doubts on these matters once and for all. It was very clear to them that they wanted no taxes either for churches or for the schools of churches. They proceeded to say just that in the state constitutional provisions on church-state. They sought to make it crystal clear that the funds of the taxpayers were not to be divided with denominational schools, but were to go exclusively to the nonsectarian, public schools which were specifically required of every state entering the Union. Consider, for example, the language of the church-state provisions in the constitution of the nation's two most populous states — New York and California.

The New York Constitution contains the following unequivocal language:

> "Neither the state nor any subdivision thereof shall use its property or credit, or any public money, or authorize or permit either to be used, directly or indirectly, in aid of maintenance, other than for examination or inspection, of any school or institution of learning wholly or in part under the direction of any religious denomination, or in which any denominational tenet or doctrine is taught. . . ."
>
> Article XI, Section 3

50

The California Constitution is equally unambiguous:

No public money shall ever be appropriated for the support of any sectarian or denominational school, or any school not under the exclusive control of the officers of the public schools; nor shall any sectarian or denominational doctrine be taught, or instruction thereon be permitted, directly or indirectly, in any of the common schools of this State.

Article IX, Section 8

Other state constitutions are likewise emphatic:

Alaska: "Schools and institutions (of the State) so established shall be free of sectarian control. No money shall be paid from public funds for the direct benefit of any religious or other private educational institution."

Article VII, Section 1

Colorado: Neither the general assembly, nor any county, city, town, township, shall district or other public corporation, shall ever make any appropriation, or pay from any public fund or moneys whatever, anything in aid of any church or sectarian society, or for any sectarian purpose, or to help support or sustain any school, academy, seminary, college, university or other literary or scientific institution, controlled by any church or sectarian denomination whatsoever; nor shall any grant or donation of land, money, or other personal property, ever be made by the state, or any such public corporation, to any church, or for any sectarian purpose.

Article IX, Section 7

Florida: No law shall be enacted authorizing the diversion or the lending of any County or District School Funds, or the appropriation of any part of the permanent or available school Fund to any other than school purposes, nor shall the same, or any part thereof, be appropriated to or used for the support of any sectarian school.

Article XII Section 13

Idaho: Neither the legislature, nor any county, city, town, township, school district, or other public corporation, shall ever make any appropriation or pay from any public fund or moneys whatever, anything in aid of any church or sectarian or religious society, or for any sectarian or religious purpose, or

51

to help support or sustain any school, academy, seminary, college, university, or other literary or scientific institution, controlled by any church, sectarian or religious denomination whatsoever; nor shall any grant or donation of land, money or other personal property ever be made by the state, or any such public corporation to any church, or for any sectarian or religious purpose.

Article IX, Section 5

Oklahoma: No public money or property shall ever be appropriated, applied, donated, or used, directly or indirectly, for the use, benefit or support of any sect, church, denomination, or system of religion, or for the use, benefit, or support of any priest, preacher, minister, or other religious teacher or dignitary, or sectarian institution as such.

Article II, Section 5

Pennsylvania: No appropriation shall be made to any charitable or educational institution not under the absolute control of the Commonwealth. . . .

Article III, Section 17

This is the way the state constitutions express it. Surely their meaning is clear. The drafters of these provisions were bent on barring all public subsidies to churches or church schools. It would be hard to compose provisions more direct and comprehensive than these. Their composers were spelling out what they conceived to be the basic premise of the First Amendment — that the people must never be taxed to support religion. Still more, they were seeking to insure that all public funds for education would be spent on the public schools.

Why did they do it? Was it because of hostility to religion? Were they trying to impose curbs on religion and reduce its scope and influence? Hardly, for the same constitutions which forbade public subsidy to religion also contained provisions guaranteeing its free exercise. In their view the two concepts belonged together. No coerced support and free exercise were complementary. The essence of free exercise of religion was voluntary support of religion. To tax the people for reigion was a contradiction. What they freely chose they would voluntarily support. Where religion was concerned they were to be free to do as they would.

52

With the passage of the Elementary and Secondary Education Act, the Higher Education Facilities Act, the National Defense Education Act, and other federal legislation of the 1960s, tax money, for the first time in our history, began to be used in various ways for church institutions. This procedure flatly contradicted the First Amendment to the Federal Constitution, both in its legislative history and in decisions of the Supreme Court. But if it contradicted the First Amendment, it outraged and trampled upon most of the state constitutions. These instruments flatly forbid the very thing the federal officials were doing. If it required some deft footwork to get around the First Amendment for aid programs of this kind, how infinitely more difficult to circumvent these painfully specific strictures of the states! The task of selling the idea that black is really white could have been no more difficult than the business of finding a way through or around these state provisions in order to subsidize church institutions.

As we have seen, the federal programs put the state officials in an embarrassing position. The federal authority was directing them to do that which their oath to uphold their state constitutions forbade them to do. Furthermore, the federal officials were able to wield the money club. If these officials would not share the federal money with parochial schools, the money would be withdrawn or would be channeled directly to the parochials in spite of them. The lot of the public school officials was not an enviable one.

For an example, consider the situation in Nebraska where a tight article of the constitution flatly forbids "any appropriation from any public fund . . . in aid of any sectarian or denominational school . . . or any educational institution which is not exclusively owned and controlled by the state or by a governmental subdivision thereof." Bound by provisions of this kind, the Nebraska Department of Education never distributed certain federal funds under ESEA to parochial schools. There was, in fact, an attorney general's ruling that this was prohibited by the State's constitution. But the Rev. John Flynn, director of education for the Catholic archdiocese of Omaha, publicly protested denial of these funds to parochial schools of his church. It was revealed by the Omaha *World-Herald*, April 26, 1970 that the archdiocesan authorities failed to endorse the "sign-off slips" for Title I aid. These slips indicate that parochial school officials are satisfied with administration of the program. It took a constitutional amendment to bring Nebraska into line.

When the Massachusetts Legislature undertook to pass some laws aiding parochial schools in the ESEA manner, it was confronted with a sweeping advisory opinion of the Commonwealth's Supreme Judicial Court which barred the way. The present provision of the constitution reads:

> . . . No grant, appropriation or use of public money or property . . . shall be made or authorized by the commonwealth or any political division thereof for the purpose of founding, maintaining, or aiding any school or institution of learning . . . which is not publicly owned and under the exclusive control, order and superintendence of public officers. . . .

On the basis of this stipulation the seven Massachusetts justices held that "the language unquestonably was designed to preclude entirely aid to all nonpublic institutions from appropriated funds. . . ." They added that the provision "constitutes a binding constitutional restraint upon the General Court and upon us until and unless it is changed by some method permitted by the Constitution of the Commonwealth."

As soon as the opinion was announced, the legislature took steps to amend the constitution. Meeting as a joint constitutional convention, that body undertook to overturn the existing ban on aid to church schools by approving an amendment which would grant the legislature authority "to make grants-in-aid to private educational institutions." This amendment, if ultimately approved by the voters in referendum, would arm the legislature with authority to effect the complete subversion of the previous provision. Subject only to the First and Fourteenth Amendments to the Federal Constitution, the Commonwealth of Massachusetts would then be free to subsidize church schools as it chose.

Federal spending was used by Robert C. Courtemanche, administrator of the Long Island, New York, Episcopal Diocese as an argument to override state constitutional provisions on church and state. His point was that the New York State Constitution should be changed in order to permit federal-type aid to parochial schools.

54

Newsday, May 18, 1970, quoted him as saying: "Funds are being given to private schools anyway and I feel it would be a shame if New York State's schools were made ineligible for some federal money because of Blaine (Article XI, Section 3)."

One result of the federal programs that could certainly have been foreseen was a powerful stimulation to clerical hopes for state subsidies to religion. Not since the Catholic Bishop Hughes waged his campaign for public subsidies in New York State in the 1840s and the drive of Catholic Archbishop LeFevre of Detroit in the 1850s had there been a major effort to pass such legislation in a state. But with the passage of federal aid to education that included parochial schools, church officials took heart. They actively resumed a battle long dormant — a battle for state subsidies to church schools. The strategy here was to use the weight of federal precedent to break down and nullify the state prohibitions.

The churchmen were over optimistic. They over estimated the impact of federal aid to parochial schools on the states. The classic miscalculation was that of Cardinal Francis Spellman of New York who felt the time was ripe to wipe out what he viewed as archaic restrictions on public aid to church institutions in the states. He determined to tackle the problem head-on and passed the word which set off a massive assault on Article XI, Section 3 of the New York State Constitution. The Cardinal thought that the big moment for his church has arrived. He thought that with an astutely planned public relations campaign the public could be sold on paying taxes for Catholic schools.

The Cardinal totally miscalculated. Perhaps this was inevitable. Surrounded as such highly placed ecclesiastics invariably are with a cabal of yes-men, it is difficult for them to understand the public mind and to anticipate the public reaction. Actually, the idea of paying taxes for church schools is not one that appeals to the public. It has to be sold with many deceptive devices and there is always the chance that the public may really understand what is at stake. If that happens, public aid to parochial schools — "parochiaid" — is dead. Fortunately for the public, though unfortunately for Cardinal Spellman and his colleagues, that is what happened in New York in 1967.

The best account of the plan to scuttle church-state separation in New York has been provided by Edd Doerr in his "Conspiracy That Failed." Doerr described the trick strategy by which the repeal of strict church-state separation in the New York Constitution (Article XI, Section 3) was sought:

> (The clerical propagandists) try to avoid talking about even indirect aid to church schools, preferring to make innocent sounding noises about "aiding children wherever they happen to attend school" or "discrimination against children seeking a God-centered education."

The entire campaign in New York featured slick pleas for "little children who are being denied their rights." One of the principal Catholic fronts operating in the campaign had the interesting name Citizens for Educational Freedom. It turned out that their idea of educational freedom was to pass laws forcing all citizens to pay taxes for Catholic schools. The real purpose of the hierarchy's campaign in New York State was not to help little children but to remove the barrier which protects New York citizens from paying taxes for the support of religious schools. The nature of the propaganda they used is indicated by the title of a folder widely circulated by CEF. It was called: *Children Are the Issue: A Question and Answer Guide to Some of the Problems Relative to Religiously Affiliated Education in the State of New York.* Another title put out by the Committee of Nonpublic School Officials of New York City: *Nearly a Million Children: A Question of Education, Not Religion.*

Commenting on what was going on, Doerr wrote:

> They make a show of professing to believe in church-state separation, religious freedom and public education while at the same time using a legal fiction (child benefit) to subvert these basic pillars of a democratic society. They know the "child benefit" concept is but a subterfuge to disguise the channeling of public aid to church schools for nonpublic, ecclesiastical purposes, with the child and his parents serving as a convenient pipeline from the public treasury to that part of the church schools which is devoted to a program of combined education and religious indoctrination.[2]

Occasionally, the clerical slip would show. Joan Prescott,

writing in the *Rockland County Journal News*, Nyack N.Y., June 1, 1967, describes a series of mass meetings sponsored by the Catholic archdiocese in a ten-county area. She reports that clerics sought to whip up the drive against Article XI, Section 3 by telling the crowd that the outcome of the battle "may mean the life or death of the Catholic Church in America." She reported that Rev. Patrick Kelleher of St. Augustine's parish in New York City told his hearers that Catholic schools in New York would be forced to close by the year 2000 unless they could get rid of Article XI, Section 3 and thereby make possible substantial state aid. Rev. Kelleher described Citizens for Educational Freedom as "the one organization that can save the Catholic school in New York State."

The decisive factor in the defeat of the clerical plans for New York State was a gimmick which overdid "child benefit" and brought a hostile reaction to the whole propaganda campaign. A series of full-page ads in many newspapers of the state boomeranged on the clerics in a tide of hostile public opinion. In order to evoke sympathy and support for the deletion of Article XI, Section 3, CEF inserted the fatal ads featuring pictures of little children allegedly suffering discrimination because of this nasty feature of the constitution. The ads showed a girl with a speech defect, another child denied psychological counseling, still another denied remedial reading aid — all because these children attended parochial schools and were shut out by the statute.

Here was the technique of the big lie and, as so often in the past, it failed. The lie was quickly pegged by Americans United which pointed out that such services were available to all children. The American Civil Liberties Union took up the matter in a statement issued Oct. 30, 1967. The statement denounced the ads as a "false and scurrilous campaign which is purposefully misleading." Florence Flast, president of the United Parents Association, stated that in New York City during the last school year 6,965 nonpublic school students received speech therapy; 11,742 received remedial reading; and 10,368 received psychological guidance. In the driver guidance program all students had been served, but no breakdown had been kept as to public and nonpublic. In other words, the charges were completely false not only in their way of stating the case but also in the facts themselves. Mrs. Flast accurately described them as the "technique of the Big Lie."

This was even too much for the ultra-liberal Protestant journal *Christianity and Crisis*. Up to that point, this journal had faithfully followed the clerical line, basing its position on ecumenical considerations. Now it protested and announced that it was "both amazed and chagrined" at the "Catholic power play."

Another trick of the parochial protagonists was to label the constitutional provision which stood in their way as the Blaine Amendment. This by a process of innuendo and leer was built up into an image of something very bad which all right-minded people would inevitably reject. Why did they coin the expression Blaine Amendment to describe Article XI, Section 3? Blaine had been dead and gone before this item was considered for the New York Constitution. The name had a bad connotation for New York Catholics who had been carefully briefed about a little episode which took place in the Presidential campaign of 1884 when James G. Blaine was the Republican nominee. Not Blaine at all, but one Samuel D. Burchard who was an early speaker at one of the Blaine rallies that year, described the Democratic Party as the Party of "Rum, Romanism and Rebellin." This catchy alliteration was widely quoted and, in time, was even ascribed to Blaine himself. The propagandists sought to tap this residue of prejudice by attaching the name of Blaine to constitutional church-state separation which they were assaulting.

It is true that James G. Blaine as a senator did advocate a constitutional amendment which would make binding the First Amendment strictures of no-establishment and free exercise on all the states. But this was only what President Ulysses S. Grant and the great majority of Congress favored and what, as it turned out, three-fourths of the New York voters favored. It was simply the American tradition of church-state separation that religion should be free and voluntary and neither inhibited nor subsidized by government. Yet, in the 1967 constitutional battle in New York State the clerical propagandists sought to portray this as something laden with discrimination and evil.

In the initial phases of the struggle the separationists had no chance. The clerical forces got to the members of the Constitutional Convention before they were ever voted on and were able to announce that they had a substantial majority committed to scuttle Article XI, Section 3. This turned out to be no idle boast. Convention President Anthony J. Travia (since appointed a federal judge) was their man all the way. A constituent who sent Mr. Travia a letter urging him to oppose deletion of Article XI, Section 3, received a form letter in reply which said:

> May I take this opportunity to acknowledge receipt of the petition . . . urging me to support the repeal of the Blaine Amendment. . . . Be advised, as I have stated on many occasions, that I favor the repeal of the Blaine Amendment and will exert my best efforts at the Convention to effectuate this change. . .[3]

The convention quickly made its decision to delete the statute by a vote of 132 to 49, leaving only the more vague and general language of the First Amendment to protect the people.

The redemptive feature in the New York situation turned out to be the referendum provision. Had the decision been left to the politicians, it is obvious what would have happened. The people's protection against the tax for religion would have simply vanished and the taxpayers would have had to contemplate a dreary succession of growing demands by clerics for public subsidy of their institutions. Many of the big names in New York politics were successfully brought into line by the clerical lobbyists. In addition to Conference President Travia, they had Gov. Nelson Rockefeller, the two senators, Robert F. Kennedy and Jacob Javits, and the Majority Leader of the New York Senate, Earl Brydges, New York City Council President Frank O'Connor and, for good measure, the Presidents of New York, Columbia, Cornell, Rochester, Syracuse Universities, and the New York State AFL-CIO. The protection of the statute remained not because of politicians but in spite of them. It remained because the people had a chance to express their own views in referendum.

When the Constitutional Convention convened there was really no problem about Article XI, Section 3. Voicces like that of Donald Harrington received scant attention. It was all assured in advance that the statute was to go; it was just a question of how to do it. Should it be put to the voters as a separate item or, should it be made a part of the total package? Gov. Rockefeller had urged that it be voted on separately, but Cardinal Spellman was against this. He knew quite well that if the separation issue were isolated in a separate item where it would stand out and be considered on its own, it would have no chance. Its only chance lay in burying it in the midst of the new constitution which would contain many "goodies" for many groups. (This was the way Convention President Travia expressed it.) Here, too, the Cardinal had his way. The new and weakened church-state section was incorporated into the constitution and all was put to the voters in a single package.

The trouble was that the church-state issue could not really be hidden. It was simply too big. A study of the newspapers during this period shows that the church-state issue figured far more prominently than any other. The issue of higher taxes was involved in the controversy, but this, too, had a reference to the church-state business. The church-state matter was discussed and debated to such an extent that it is quite fair to say that the referendum really hung on this issue: did the New York electorate want to ease their church-state separation and open the way for tax support of church institutions?

With such an issue clearly posed, the response of the religious communities was decisive. Despite the progress of the ecumenical movement which had been counted on to nullify Protestant opposition, the leadership of these groups refused to acquiesce in the scuttling of Article XI, Section 3. Dr. Theodore Conklin, executive of the New York State Council of Churches, announced his opposition to the new charter and called on Protestants to defeat it. So did Dr. Dan Potter, executive of the New York City Protestant Council, and Episcopal Bishop Horace W.B. Donegan. Dr. Conklin was a tower of strength in the battle against the proposed constitution as was Dr. Arthur W. Mielke, minister of the great First Presbyterian Church of Buffalo.

But this was in no sense a Protestant-Catholic conflict. There was some Protestant support for Cardinal Spellman and one need only to analyze the voting on the charter to see that Catholic voters opposed the new constitution in almost the same proportion as did the Protestants. There were even Catholic volunteers to pass out the literature of Americans United for Separation of Church and State to crowds coming from Catholic masses.

Yet the fact remains that the ruling hierarchy of the Roman Catholic Church led a strong effort to win the referendum for the "Blainelsss" constitution. Although forbidden by the terms of its tax exemption to engage in lobbying or legislative activity to any substantial degree, these clerics poured millions of dollars and thousands of man-hours into their drive. *Newsweek* (Nov. 6, 1967) declared that the Catholic drive to eliminate Article XI, Section 3 had a budget "estimated as high as $2 million." The CEF, a Catholic action group, is reported to have spent over $900,000 with one advertising firm — Boyce, Smith and Tobac. Many related groups such as Citizens for a New Constitution and Independent Citizens for a New Constitution raised and expended substantial sums.

What was the extent of the commitment by the diocesan apparatus? Parish funds were freely used in the campaigning and special assessments were levied on pastors. We are indebted to a Catholic lay group, the Laymen's Association of Brooklyn-Queens, for its exposure of the way the hierarchy operated to keep its political fund-raising a secret. This Catholic group discovered and disclosed that parish funds were being transferred to action groups such as Citizens for the New Constitution in such a way that neither the pastor's name nor the parish name would be linked to the donation. On the basis of a fact sheet circulated to all pastors it appears that pastors would draw checks "to cash" from parish funds, then have a bank check drawn payable to the action group. They were directed to have the check carry the name of an individual as donor, but not that of the church or its societies. The sheets also suggested that several checks be sent rather than one. A full account of the Laymen's Association complaint appeared in the *National Catholic Reporter* for Nov. 1, 1967. It contains the observation from the Catholic laymen that their association:

> deplores the clandestine manner in which this campaign for funds was apparently conducted. The association believes that it is unethical and improper to use for political lobbying funds donated by the faithful for specific charitable purposes . . . At no time in its recent history has the Diocese of Brooklyn marshalled its forces with such energy as in the present campaign

to seek public aid for parochial education.

As seen in retrospect, the clerical campaign to be rid of Article XI, Section 3 does not appear to have been well conceived. It was too slick, too tricky, too transparently deceptive. The press was eminently fair. It not only printed the clerical propaganda but the answering statements which tore it to ribbons. Press coverage, as well as that of the other mass media, was two-sided. In that kind of open situation the clerics could not prevail even with their own members. The final count in the referendum was 3,487,513 to 1,327,000 against the new charter. This was a 3 to 1 margin. Every county in the state and every borough in New York City voted "No." Catholic, Protestant Jewish — it seemed to make no difference. All voters united in convincing chorus that they did not want to be taxed for church schools.

As we shall see in Chapter 5, two referenda in Michigan and Nebraska in 1970 produced a similar result. The public does not favor parochiaid.

In New York State one witnessed the classic effort to set aside strict constitutional provisions for the separation of church and state. New York was perhaps unique in the amount of money expended by the church and in the thoroughness and determination with which the endeavor was pursued. But New York was only one instance among others. The late sixties and early seventies were a time of constitutional revision.

At least 15 states were, are, or shortly will be engaged in revamping their own constitutions. In everyone of them the clergy have been right on the job from the very beginning in an endeavor to remove or weaken the strictures on tax support for religious institutions and programs. For the most part, this has been, as it was in New York, primarily a Roman Catholic endeavor since the clergy of this church are concerned to get subsidies for their failing school system. However, in a state like Michigan where there is a sectarian push to pass church school subsidy bills, we find some Protestant and Jewish groups joining in the drive.

How the clergy operate in these situations can be seen in the case of Virginia. The clerical power in Virginia was not nearly so

62

formidable as in New York. Nor did the Richmond diocese possess the vast financial resources necessary for a statewide campaign to remove from the constitution an offending section which forbids a tax "for the support of any church or ministry." Or the even more sweeping provision: "No appropriation of public funds shall be made to any school or institution now owned or exclusively controlled by the State or some political subdivision thereof. . . ."(Let it be noted, too, that a later provision which did permit state aid to private schools specifically excluded such aid to "sectarian schools.") Accordingly, the church leadership undertook a low key campaign pitched to the tune of helping "handicapped children." It marshalled its forces behind a single amendment which would enable public funds to be given to church schools for the "education or training of emotionally disturbed, mentally retarded, and mentally and physically handicapped Virginia students and such other handicapped Virginia students as may be prescribed by law. . . ."

The brilliance of this maneuver cannot be doubted. Hardly anything else would have had a chance in Virginia. One has only to acquaint himself with the manner in which the Federal Government handles the concept of handicapped to realize how broad this permissiveness could be. As the term has been used, and as it is used in the proposed amendment, this word could be stretched to include virtually anyone. Furthermore, there was no limitation imposed on the kind of teaching that could be subsidized in the church school. Not a word proscribing nonsectarian teaching. Not a word limiting the aid to secular subjects. Thus, by an innocuous appearing amendment, churches would be authorized to draw tax support not only for their schools in general, but for the strictly religious training of such institutions. This amendment envisaged a tax for religion. The fact that it would be taxation for the religious institutions and training of people who are labeled handicapped was of little significance. As CHURCH & STATE commented: "It is just as 'sinful and tyrannical' to use Jefferson's phrase, for the state to force citizens to support the religion of handicapped people as of any other part of the population."[4]

A steady stream of witnesses representing Catholic interests supported this amendment. They supported it on humanitarian grounds: surely church-state matters should not interfere with the care of the unfortunate. They seemed to view as irrelevant the fact that Virginia already had an excellent public program for serving the handicapped and one quite capable of further expansion. On the ground that the churchmen had not fought the church-state provisions elsewhere in the constitution and were only making this plea for handicapped children, the concession was made. But citizens groups would not have it so. There was an instant reaction throughout the state. Spearheaded by Americans United, a powerful citizens' consensus demanded, and eventually got, a reversal of the decision. Amendment 25 was eliminated in what can only be regarded as a great victory for religious freedom. Again, the people spoke and their voice was heard.

Another bitter struggle developed in New Mexico in 1969 when that state's constitution was under revision. Antagonists in the struggle were the Santa Fe Archdiocese of the Catholic Church and the Albuquerque Chapter of Americans United. When the Constitutional Convention convened there was immediately placed before the delegates a church-state proposal previously drafted by a special Constitutional Revision Commission. This proposal included language barring direct public grants to church schools but which would have permitted such forms of indirect aid as tuition grants or vouchers, purchase of contracting for educational services from such schools, shared time programs, etc.

At the first hearing on the religious liberty provisions the clerical advocates of the new provision were out in force. They claimed there was no difference between the old provision which flatly forbade use of public funds for church schools and the proposed provision which would have permitted assistance of various kinds. The Catholic Archbishop of Santa Fe, John Peter Davis, had been transferred from Puerto Rico as a result of a political clash with former Governor Munoz Marin. His comment on the constitutional situation in New Mexico: "I think the wall of separation of church and state is a figment of the imagination, a fiction of law. I say walls should come down."

The archbishop did his best to bring the wall down by tapping the state for support of his denomination's parish schools. But effectively opposing the diocese and meeting every argument was the Albuquerque Chapter of Americans United headed by Alan

Dale Danielson, Rev. J.R. Burnett, Thomas E. Bowser, Jay D. Anderson and H.C. Reavis. Educational materials were widely distributed, excellent presentations were made at the hearings. The mass media gave space not only to the anti-separationists but also to the pro-separationists. The result was a constitution whose church-state provisions were eminently satisfactory to the separationists. The strictures of the old constitution were carried over into the new as the clerical leaders were discomfited. Eventually, the proposed instrument was defeated in referendum on other grounds by a margin of about 2,000 votes. This meant the old constitution with its church-state provisions was still in force in New Mexico.

An earlier test (1968) found the clerics seeking to emasculate the strong church-state provisions of the Florida Constitution. Again there was a grim struggle as churchmen undertook to loosen the tight provisions against state subsidy to church institutions. Again the churchmen suffered defeat to their ambitions, though by the narrowest of margins. The language which survived the determined onslaught of the Catholic clergy reads:

No revenue of the state or any political subdivision or agency thereof shall ever be taken from the public treasury directly or indirectly in aid of any church, sect or religious denomination or in aid of any sectarian institution.

As has now been indicated, the endeavors of churchmen to change constitutional provisions of the states governing church-state relations have not proved productive. The reason is quite simple: it is highly difficult to conceal the real intent. There is something about a constitutional change which impresses the people as highly significant and decisive. Laws come and go. They can be passed one year and repealed the next. But a constitution conveys the aura of permanence. At this point the voters tend to be more than ordinarily conservative. There is also the matter of taxes. Their taxes are so stiff already that any new provision which carries even a hint of raising them some more is marked for defeat. Taxpayers do not want to add the expenses of church schools to their staggering burden. They are not gullible enough to accept the argument that parochial schools save the public money and are therefore entitled to public subsidy. If these schools are to receive subsidy, where is the saving? Finally, the people, most of them, really believe in the separation of church and state. If the churches have done as well as they have over the last century-and-a-half without tax support, they feel that they can continue without it.

The church drive for constitutional change can be regarded as a failure born of a clerical misunderstanding of popular sentiment. The effort will, of course, continue but there appears to be little likelihood of its success save possibly in a state like Massachusetts where clerical power is admittedly great. The church has hit upon an alternative approach which has already proved far more productive. The new idea is simply to circumvent the state constitutional provisions in much the same way that federal legislation has circumvented the First Amendment. Admittedly, the task is much harder in the states because as we have seen, the prohibitions are more specific. But the churchmen soon came to realize that evasive stratagems for aiding church schools indirectly were their best means of nullifying the state provisions.

State legislators were urged to get in line with the federal programs. As Msgr. Francis J. Harrison, dean of the Binghamton-Endicott-Johnson City, N.Y. Catholic clergy put it: "(The New York Assembly) should be free to evolve a new public policy with respect to church and state in education. Separation of church and state is no longer a matter for the states to decide. The state ought to get in line with the Federal Government."[5]

If it were right for the Federal Government to help church schools, then how could it possibly be wrong for the states to do so? In fact, as we have already seen, the federal spending on parochial schools had the effect of compelling state participation in this program. If the Federal Government could provide textbooks for parochial schools, then why could not New York State do so, also?

Indeed, New York State offers a classic instance of the new clerical strategy for obtaining public money for church schools. Having been repulsed by the electorate in a frontal assault, the clerics resorted almost immediately to circumvention. New York Senate Majority Leader Earl W. Brydges was one of the original sponsors of deleting tight church-state separation from the state's constitution. Apparently he learned nothing from the 1967 referendum, for immediately thereafter he introduced Article XI,

Section 3 repeal in the New York Legislature and set the wheels in motion for another try. He did the same thing again in the 1969 legislative session. Then he seemed to have a change of heart, or rather of direction. He began to suspect that repeal was really unnecessary. They could keep the offending provisions and do an end run around them just as other states had already undertaken to do. Accordingly, Sen. Brydges stated that the repeal of Article XI, Section 3 was no longer essential.[5] He then introduced two bills which would provide state support for sectarian higher institutions of learning. The attempted circumvention lay in a stipulation that none of the state's money could be used for religious instruction, or for the advancement or inhibition of religion.

Although persisting in his position that repeal of the statute was imperative, Gov. Nelson Rockefeller agreed with Sen. Brydges that ways could be found to provide some state subsidies in the meantime. He proposed to do this and did do this at a time when he was actually cutting allocations for the public schools. The trick Gov. Rockefeller employed was described as "reimbursement for services required by the state." The reasoning was that the State of New York through its education laws imposed certain standards and requirements upon private schools. Since it would take some expenditure on their part to fulfill these requirements, the state could legally reimburse them. This particular syndrome began with a grant of $28 million in April, 1970. It provided for state payments for mandated services — payments to parochial schools for their bookkeeping and record keeping — things they would obviously have to do in any case. Sponsors of the legislation admitted there had been no study of the matter. They had just decided to give something to the parochials and the figure of $28 million seemed to be about right.

Again, there was a federal example. The Office of Education made a flat grant of $90,000 to the National Catholic Educational Association for statistical information which the government agency was compiling. It was announced that the Catholic group would cooperate in the circulation of a questionnaire.

This syndrome appeared to offer possibilities of substantial state aid. For example, the state had a requirement that all school classes must be conducted in safe and sanitary buildings. Why could not the church be paid for the construction of buildings necessary to meet this requirement? In fact, a bill providing for up-keep and maintenance of church schools was eventually passed into law in New York State. Even houses of worship might be built by the state under this logic. For these buildings, too, were subject to safety and sanitation standards imposed by the state.

The legislation was roundly condemned by Americans United for Separation of Church and State and by PEARL (Public Education and Religious Liberty), a group representing 25 New York organizations. In a statement issued April 14, 1970 PEARL pointed out that Gov. Rockefeller had met the preceding month with eight Roman Catholic bishops but had flatly refused to meet with a group opposing the legislation. "Apparently the governor is fearful that we might be able to change his mind, for he has failed even to acknowledge our request to meet with him," the statement said.

The political flavor of parochiaid can be clearly detected in Governor Rockefeller's blatant bid for the Catholic vote in his 1970 reelection campaign. He placed large advertisements in every Catholic paper in the state boasting about what all he had done for Catholic schools. "We've done a lot," the ads proclaimed. "We'll do more."

All of this makes it abundantly clear that when governors and legislators under the lash of clerical pressure seek to subvert con-stitutonal provisions, they can always find a way to do it. It may not be a very plausible way, like this one above. But a way they will find. The mandated services statute was promptly challenged in a lawsuit filed in federal court. The court eventually found the law to be in violation of the First Amendment.

Far from quitting, the parochiaid promoters came right back with a $33 million bill which financed the teaching of secular sub-jects in church schools. This bill was signed into law by Governor Rockefeller the very day the Supreme Court struck down the similar Pennsylvania law. When the New York law was likewise ruled unconstitutional, the sectarians did not quit even then. They immediately came up with a bill providing tuition grants, graduated tax credits, and also direct grants to parochial and private schools for repair and maintenance of buildings. PEARL at once challenged its constitutionality in the courts.

It is enlightening to examine the case of one typical parochial school — Our Lady of Loretto with 545 students, located in Hempstead, New York. A study of this school reported by Martin Buskin in *Newsday,* March 16, 1970, notes that while the New York Constitution forbids any government aid at all to sectarian schools, directly or indirectly, this school receives various grants totaling 28 per cent of its annual budget of $138,000. Buskin then lists the various forms of aid. Much of this is federal, but some is from the State of New York. Busing of students accounts for $14,900; free textbooks $2,000; medical and dental care of students $7,200; milk fund $150 per month; special instructor in reading $9,250; Saturday reading program $400; books and materials $732; summer remedial programs $2,000. Buskin observes that these forms of aid are held to be legal because they supposedly benefit the children rather than the religious school.

In the late sixties and early seventies major drives sparked principally by the Catholic hierarchy sought to pass some kind of legislation providing tax support for church schools in 38 states. Pennsylvania offers a case study of the kind of clerical political pressure that was exerted in these situations. The clerical operation here is especially interesting because of the provisions in the state constitution which appear to close the door tightly and finally against any state aid to church schools.

How did the Catholic Church manage to push through the Pennsylvania Legislature and persuade the governor to sign into law a bill which did provide such aid? The bill was actually drafted for the legislators by William Ball, an attorney who was then serving as the Catholic lobbyist in Harrisburg. It sought to evade the church-state strictures by a number of ruses. The bill provided for the creation of an educational authority. Pennsylvanians are familiar with this idea. They have, for example, their Turnpike Authority. These authorities have at least a semi-autonomous status apart from the state and have actually been used for some kinds of programs which the constitution forbids to the state. (Borrowing of money beyond a certin limit, for example.) They began, therefore, with an entity which was not quite the state, though it was to act for the state. This authority was given funds from a tax newly imposed on harness racing, not funds from the general revenue of the state. (This was later shifted to a tax on cigarette sales.) The authority was authorized to purchase educational services (e.g. teaching in science, mathematics, foreign languages and physical education) wherever such services were available. But these were to be only secular educational services, not religious.

The plan appears to be paper thin. The educational authority is an official agency of the state. The funds at its disposal are funds belonging to the state just as truly as any others. And, as we have already pointed out, if one feeds funds into a church or a church school, it really makes no difference which particular item of the budget is said to be fed. The budget is one and if a part of it is subsidized all of it is subsidized. As Justice Douglas once stated it:

> The most effective way to establish any institution is to finance it; and this truth is reflected in the appeals by the church groups for public funds to finance their religious schools. Financing a church either in its strictly religious activities or in its other activities is equally unconstitutional, as I understand the Establishment Clause. Budgets for one activity may be technically separable from budgets for others. But the institution is an inseparable whole, a living organism, which is strengthened in proselytizing when it is strengthened in any department by contributions from other than its own members. What may not be done directly may not be done indirectly lest the Establishment Clause become a mockery.[7]

Despite what the clergy were saying in their propaganda to the legislators and the voters, one can scarcely doubt that they regarded the state subsidies as important aid to the teaching of their religion. This is well illustrated by the following from the weekly bulletin of St. Frances Cabrini Roman Catholic Parish, Allen, Park, Michigan, October 19, 1969:

> Parochiaid would enable the parishes and parents to greatly augment and improve religious instruction for all. Church funds, which now must be used to finance government required secular subjects taught in our Catholic schools, could be freed to finance fuller scale religious education programs.

But let us concede the case for a moment and say that it is possible for the state to subsidize only the secular segment of the instruction offered in a church school. What is more important to a church school than secular instruction? Lacking adequate secular instruction, the church school would soon lose its entire opportunity for religious indoctrination. If secular instruction failed parents would no longer patronize the church school and the school might even encounter problems with public officials insisting on certain standards of performance. From any point of view, therefore, the argument that the constitutional ban on church school aid can be circumvented by aiding secular instruction only, is notoriously weak. Yet this was the very ploy used to circumvent a constitution which provides that "no money raised for the support of the public schools of the Commonwealth shall be appropriated to or used for the support of any sectarian school."

Once Mr. Ball and his colleagues of the Pennsylvania Catholic Conference had hatched the plan, the church threw its entire political strength behind it. The parish schools were used as well as the Sunday masses. Great pressures were put on Gov. Raymond P. Shafer and the legislators. Some priests sent telegrams in the names of all their parishioners and had the bills sent to the individuals whose names they had used. Parochial school students and parents flooded officials with form letters. Cardinal John J. Kroll appeared before an ecumenical gathering of Protestants to appeal for favorable consideration to some state aid for his hard-pressed denominational schools. "My personal conviction," he pleaded, "is that to the extent that religious schools fulfill the secular needs of our society, they deserve support." The bill was passed and signed into law. Years of litigation were required before the Supreme Court eventually found it unconstitutional.

In passing, we might note that the effect of this political *tour de force* on the public schools of Pennsylvania has already been felt. In order to provide a semblance of constitutionality, the Pennsylvania legislators had to include secular private schools in their plan for purchase of educational services. Such institutions were not at all loath to accept the proffered funds, whether they really needed them or not. Since the grants were pitched to what the school was already expending, some of these rich, secular schools began to draw a disproportionate share of the aid. Catholic leaders actually complained that the law had been passed to help their schools, that it was being abused and something would have to be done about it! The law was subsequently amended to suit the churchmen.

George LaNoue has pointed out that in order to fund the program of aid to private schools, the public schools have had to be cut.[8] Some ghetto children in Philadelphia attended double sessions and the school year had to be shortened due to lack of funds.

The very next year, the same group of clerics was back — not for $4.3 million this time but for $41 million. They got it, too — half that amount the first year and the full amount in succeeding years. Rep. Martin P. Mullen, original sponsor of the legislation in the Pennsylvania Legislature, predicted an ultimate figure of $75 to $80 million annually for parochial schools.

A lawsuit challenging the law as in violation of the First Amendment was dismissed by a three-judge federal court in a split decision. Two judges could see no violation in what the legislature had done. It had, they averred, acted responsibly to meet an emergency in the parochial schools. The case was appealed directly to the United States Supreme Court. Chief Justice William H. Hastie of the District Court wrote a minority opinion which held that the Pennsylvania law was in clear violation of the no-establishment clause of the First Amendment. He described the law as a legislative scheme which violates the First and Fourteenth Amendments.

In a trenchant editorial December 2, 1969, the Pittsburgh *Post-Gazette* declared:

> Obviously the state is directly helping church-related schools by relieving them of a significant part of their costs and thus enabling them to continue operating — at the taxpayers' expense. . . .
> To fulfill its obligation to education, the Legislature could have provided more funds for public schools which would have to absorb those Catholic children whose schools could not be kept open.

Eventually, the case reached the U.S. Supreme Court which unanimously struck down the Pennsylvania law, holding that because of excessive entanglement between church and state this law did offend the First Amendment. (See discussion — Chapter 6).

Perhaps the chief significance of Pennsylvania's purchase of services plan marked the end of child benefit as the favorite ruse for church school subsidies and the beginning of the secular subject gambit. The child benefit ruse featured the notion that the aid the state was giving was not to the school, only to the child in the school. The new strategy acknowledged that the aid was to the school all right but only for training in secular subjects required by the state under its compulsory education laws. That is, the state was hiring the church school to perform a secular service in education.

The facts are that child benefit had become so patently absurd that even some of its original sponsors gave up on it. The Jesuit journal, *America,* in its January 14, 1967 issue, acknowledged that "when the benefit itself is academic in character and is intended to help the child in his school work, the distinction becomes almost meaningless." The Jesuit magazine then counseled Catholics to strive forthrightly for direct government aid to church schools while abandoning "dubious distinctions between aid to school children and aid to schools."

'Ohio followed its first auxiliary services parochiaid law with a second providing basic forms of aid to church schools. Under the original legislation a long list of church school programs could be funded by the state. The second measure which the church succeeded in forcing through the legislature moved the parochials to near parity with the public school. They could pay up to 85 per cent of their teachers' salaries with public funds. The only nod to church-state separation was the stipulation that the state funds could not be used to finance the teaching of religious subjects. This was not a problem, as state money could be used to replace funds for teachers' salaries in religious subjects.

In this legislative gambit we see the adroit opening with the use of disturbed, crippled, and handicapped children followed by a drive for full subsidy for the church schools. The end result of the Ohio law is the channeling of substantial tax funds into institutions created and operated by the church for the purpose of carrying on its program of indoctrinating its young and recruiting its clergy.

The reaction of the Ohio Catholic clergy was understandably jubilant. They rightly recognized the substantial contribution from the state which Gov. James A. Rhodes, a Presbyterian, had succeeded in making available for their church. They feted him at

73

a gathering of parochial school officials and even inserted at considerable cost large ads in Cleveland's daily papers explaining the great work that the governor had done. At the conclave Gov. Rhodes acknowledged the tributes with the observation that Ohio was leading the nation in support given to nonpublic schools. The governor also was received and commended by the Pope.

As might have been anticipated, the Catholic diocesan organization became a bastion of political support for Governor Rhodes when he announced for the U.S. Senate. Msgr. William N. Novicky, superintendent of Cleveland Catholic schools, set up a campaign dinner for Governor Rhodes. He explained the matter to his colleagues: "We are only beginning our struggle for equal distribution of school monies. Let it be known that the nonpublic school children and parents appreciate the leadership of Governor Rhodes."

The effects of the parochiaid law were soon felt. Funding of the parochial schools meant curtailment of public school funds. A dramatic instance of what this could mean was provided by the Waterloo School District, Randolph, Ohio, where three public schools were forced to close in the fall of 1969. "We just ran out of money," explained Superintendent Clyde Quimby. "We're $43,000 in the hole right now." According to the *Christian Science Monitor*, November 26, 1969, some 19,000 pupils in 40 elementary and secondary schools faced the prospect of a shutdown. The Youngstown schools were also forced to shut down and Cincinnati was threatened. Explanation: — no money. Directly responsible was the diversion of large sums to the church schools.

While Governor Rhodes exulted that Ohio was providing more funds for parochial schools than any other state, he failed to mention that Ohio ranked 47th among the states in aid provided for public schools. The Ohio parochiaid law was eventually struck down by a federal District Court as we shall see in Chapter 6, but it had its influence on the legislatures of many states.

The Pennsylvania law served as a model not only for the Ohio law but also for similar laws in Rhode Island and Connecticut, Louisiana and New Jersey. All provided public funds for direct grants to church schools. In Connecticut, for example, $6 million a year was spent on 360 private schools, 90 per cent of them Roman

74

Catholic. These states used the Pennsylvania rationale carefully devised by William Ball in collaboration with attorneys of the United States Catholic Conference. The aid was supposed to be for the secular courses offered by the school, principally in supplementing salaries of lay teachers. The constitutionality of all three laws was promptly challenged in the courts by Americans United for Separation of Church and State, the American Civil Liberties Union, the American Jewish Congress, state educational bodies, and other plaintiffs. The eventual outcome was the striking down by the courts of the entire purchase of services stratagem for aiding church schools.

Perhaps the most illuminating instance of the sectarian quest for public subsidy was one that took place in Michigan. In no other states, with the possible exceptions of Illinois and Pennsylvania, did Catholic Action undertake a blitz so thorough and emphatic. The ostensible planner was Citizens for Educational Freedom, a Catholic front group which, in Michigan, had the aid of a strong sector within the Christian Reformed Church. This group had also invested heavily in private, sectarian schools. A carefully drawn battle plan was prepared and distributed by a predominantly Catholic group called the Michigan Association of Non-Public Schools. The announced objective was an immediate $40 million grant to parochial schools patterned after the Pennsylvania law. But the committee actually endorsed a plan under which the state would increase its support of parochials by 10 per cent a year until 100 per cent of state aid was achieved.

Along with a definitive statement on Catholic education by the Catholic Bishops of Michigan, the battle plan included a timetable of day by day activities to be maintained from the very beginning of the legislative session to the target day for passage of the bill into law. The objective for April, to give an example, was "a steady, continuous flow of personal, well-articulated letters" to state officials. Dated letters with the month and year only were to be collected by local chairmen and mailed at proper intervals, thus insuring "regularity and a steady increase in volume." The May and June program was to focus on the governor and senators since by that time the bill was supposed to have been through the House. Activities were to include sending "one or two carloads of women" from each parish each week to meet with their senator. These groups were to assume responsibility for getting 200 letters to their senator and 100 to the governor.

Climaxing the passage of the legislation which the leaders regarded as certain, they envisaged a victory banquet with the archbishop in attendance along with the legislators who had been prominent in securing the bill's passage. "Gifts of Appreciation" were to be distributed as gracious speeches of thanks were made.

In a sharply worded letter addressed to Bishop Thomas J. Gumbleton of Detroit, John P. Yorke, president of the Detroit Association of (Catholic) Laymen, admonished: "In the name of decency and fairness, we insist that you refrain from the threatening and devious tactics being used in an attempt to bludgeon the Legislature into passing the parochiaid portion of Governor Milliken's educational reform package."

Despite this massive effort by the clerical forces, the 1968-69 session of the Michigan Legislature failed to pass the Catholic bill. Undaunted, these same people went right back to work as the 1969-70 session got underway. Eventually the bill did pass in 1970 and was signed into law. It put the parochial schools into the basic education budget of the state. The new law was nullified by a referendum which amended the state's constitution to bar such forms of parochial school aid as the law had provided.

Moving beyond child benefit and special services, clerical pressure groups are today pressing the case for direct public subsidy in at least 38 states. Defeated or sidetracked in one legislative session, they are back at the next. We should recall that the various state constitutional bans on public aid to church schools had at least a two-fold purpose. They were included in these instruments not only to insure separation of church and state and to defend the people against a tax for religion, but also to protect the funds of the public schools.

As we have already seen, the clerical protagonists sought in a few instances to set these provisions aside by direct attempts to amend the state constitution. Nebraska voters overwhelmingly defeated such a proposal in 1970. Michigan voters in the same year approved a tight church-state amendment which bars every form of aid to church schools except transportation. The fate of a proposal to delete church-state separation from the New York State Charter has been noted.

Generally speaking, attempts at constitutional amendment have been the exception. Easier, more appealing and more successful, is the end run around the constitutional provisions. The clerics seek by some strategy of indirection to do what the constitutions forbid.

The state battles for "parochiaid" have taken on the character of a nationwide drive for church school aid legislation. Witness the battle plan prepared by the United States Catholic Conference and sent to all dioceses and archdioceses in the country. It is dated November 14, 1969. The plan bears the imprimatur of the United States Catholic Conference and is signed by William R. Consedine, chief lobbyist for the Conference in Washington, D.C. It deals with 38 states, describing in detail exactly what the church hopes to achieve in the way of church school subsidies in each. The plan is an information piece and a summons to action addressed to state Catholic Conferences, church lobbyists, church education leaders and other leaders who are concerned with the outcomes.

The battles for church school subsidies in the 38 states follow rather closely the pattern set in Pennsylvania. The program calls for the hiring of professional lobbyists knowledgeable in the legislative techniques of each particular state. Also for the mounting of a statewide propaganda effort via the mass media. The propaganda stresses the difficult financial plight of the Catholic schools without, however, ever submitting an audited financial statement to prove the case. The publicity also threatens that Catholic schools may have to close up and dump their children on the public schools. Parochial schools and masses are used to mount massive letter-writing and telegram-sending campaigns centering on the governor and members of the legislature. Catholic Action groups like Citizens for Educational Freedom and the Knights of Columbus are brought into the campaign. No possible angle of pressure and propaganda is overlooked. Lawyers hired by the Catholic Conference even draft the proposed church school aid legislation. Once the legislation is passed, the Catholic lawyers lead the defense of its constitutionality.

One of the most amazing exploits was that of the San Antonio archdiocese which hired as its chief lobbyist Joe J. Bernal, a senator in the Texas State Legislature. Thus it assured itself of at least one favorable vote! Apparently Texas has no conflict of interest legislation which would cover even as crass a matter as this. Senator Bernal reportedly drew around $20,000 from the archdiocese in addition to his salary as a senator. This was disclosed in Paul Thompson's story in the *San Antonio Evening News*, Feb. 26, 1970.

The Roman Catholic Church is undoubtedly investing millions of dollars in this mighty legislative effort in the 38 states. This church, like all other C-3 organizations, is barred by law from expending any substantial portion of its income on political or legislative action. The Internal Revenue Service has moved against one small organization after another, canceling their tax exemptions, for alleged violations of this provision of the tax law. The Catholic Church openly flouts the law, admittedly spends vast sums in lobbying and legislative programs and is never even questioned. This church can and does violate the law with impunity. It realizes that substantial expenditures to pass laws now can mean a lucrative income of billions from tax funds in the long years to come. Here is a sample of the kind of political direction that was provided by clerics in the Pennsylvania parochial subsidy campaign. These are the words of Msgr. Edward T. Hughes, a political lobbyist as well as director of the Philadelphia archdiocesan schools:

> Speaking bluntly, I do not believe any concerned Catholic parent can vote responsibly unless he knows the position of his legislator on the critical question of state aid to nonpublic school children. I say to every parent of a child in a Catholic school, examine the record of your candidate for the Pennsylvania legislature and consider their stand on (this) question . . . If we shirk our responsibility now, let us give up all hope of any further aid for our children.

A few additional samples of the clerical legislative program now being pressed around the nation are here provided. The diocese of Rockville Centre, N.Y., early in 1970 sent out to all its members a stiff admonition to get their letters in to the state legislators promptly. Quotas of forty addressed and stamped letters were provided for each member of the action committee who was required to get the letters written, enclosed and returned to the area chairmen who would tally and mail them. In order to insure a variety of texts, various suggested forms were offered. The communication urged: "Please write *one* original letter using sample letters as a guide and write same to each legislator listed — forty letters in all."

In New York City, clergymen favoring state subsidy to religious schools seized upon local elections for trustees in public school districts. There had been sentiment in New York to have district autonomy in school management on the theory that this would create local interest and pride in the schools. But at the very first elections the clergy entered the picture with their disciplined corps of block voters. The result was a large contingent of priests, nuns, rabbis, and parents of parochial school students were elected as trustees. These persons had no interest whatever in the public schools. They were concerned solely with the parochial and Hebrew day schools and with obtaining tax funds for such institutions. The fate of the public schools under their management will be easy to conjecture. The political tactics of the religious groups were decried by parents' groups who suggested that they would embitter community relations.

An effort by the Hartford archdiocese to conceal its lobbying activities in Connecticut brought a citizens' complaint to the attorney general. The story as told in the *Hartford Courant*, Jan. 24, 1970, involved a payment of $59,950 by the archdiocese — "the highest fee ever paid an agent working the Capitol beat." What drew the ire of Mrs. Eleanor Taft Tilton and her associates was the fact that the archdiocese did not register its lobby as required by state law, but tried to hide behind its paid agent, a Madison Avenue group known as Burke and Corbin Associations. Mrs. Tilton contended that instead of listing Gene Burke, the church should have been listed since it paid the fee. Msgr. James A. Connelly, secretary-treasurer of the Catholic Committee on Education, said that the Burke firm was not hired to lobby but only to prepare reports and surveys. The attorney general ruled that the listing of Gene Burke satisfied the requirements of the law. In any case the expenditure of $59,950 plus added thousands in political costs did result in a law providing an initial $6 million annually for the parish schools. When one calculates that this breakthrough did no more than open the public treasury to the church and that the opening could be widened again and again by successful legislative forays, the entire operation can be described as profitable indeed.

In fact, the dust had not even settled from the previous skirmish when the Catholic lobby in Connecticut was back for more. A pastoral letter was read in Sunday masses at the state's 360 churches saying: "We urge you to tell your own elected state senator and state representative, preferably through a brief letter written today, your convictions in support of a bill that provides to nonpublic schools the substantial financial help they deserve."

In Illinois, a statewide lobbying campaign called "The Time for Action" was initiated with Martin J. McLaughlin as co-ordinator. Chief lobbyist for the Chicago archdiocese was the Rev. James F. Moriarty. A film also called "The Time for Action" was prepared and distributed. The purpose of the legislative effort was "to inform every Illinois citizen of the quality and value of non-public education and to mobilize support for legislation to aid (these schools) in Illinois."

In Massachusetts, the Boston archdiocese hired lobbyist William B. Ball, to draft a church school aid bill, just as the Philadelphia archdiocese had previously done. Mr. Ball's bill, patterned on his earlier product, would enable the state to "finance the purchase of secular educational services from nonpublic schools." This meant in practice that the State of Massachusetts would pay the salaries of parochial school teachers. The four Massachusetts dioceses quickly endorsed the Ball bill stating that it had been introduced at their behest.

In Kentucky, the state's Catholic Conference with a battery of clerical lobbyists headed by the Rev. Thomas P. Casper, superintendent of the Louisville archdiocesan schools, and the Rev. John V. Hevenauer, superintendent of schools of the Covington diocese, descended on the State Capitol and beseiged legislators for state aid. In Missouri, Catholic bishops set up an action organization called MANS (Missouri Association of Nonpublic Schools) to press the campaign on behalf of parish schools. A parish-by-parish organization was formed to coordinate the political effort in the legislature. The first thing the group did was to slap two notices on the desks of the legislators as they assembled for their 75th General

Assembly. The first asserted that Catholic schools of the state deserved compensation for the secular education they were providing for 16 per cent of Missouri's school children. The second said that unless they got some aid at the 1969 session they would recommend closing down all their grade and high schools September 1, 1969. We should note in passing that they neither got the aid nor closed the schools. But they were soon making a new move with the old threat. Said James Powers, chairman of MANS, "Never before have the Catholics in Missouri been so organized."

In Florida, churchmen had been frustrated in an earlier attempt to change the church-state provisions of the constitution. Now the bishops hired a capable staff of lobbyists in Tallahassee and waged a vigorous legislative affort to pass an aid bill which appeared unconstitutional on the face. As might have been anticipated, this campaign called into being an answering campaign sparked by Americans United for Separation of Church and State and spearheaded by a wide representation of churchmen, educators, parent-teachers groups, and others concerned for separation of church and state.

According to the *San Antonio Express*, February 12, 1970, the Texas bishops not only hired a member of the State Senate as lobbyist but also set up a statewide legislative effort headed by Col. Joseph McShane. Said Col. McShane: "We will be ascertaining from those nominees — candidates for public office in Austin — how they feel about state aid for private schools." Col. McShane stated flatly that the Catholic bishops "have joined together for a campaign" to make state aid an issue in "the 1971 session of the state legislature." It was announced that the head of the drive would be Archbishop Francis J. Furey of San Antonio.

In Louisiana a comparable effort forced a "parochiaid" bill through the 1970 legislature and another in 1972.

While the main burden of the campaign planning and the actual lobbying necessarily had to be carried by the dioceses, the United States Catholic Conference rendered many kinds of useful assistance. It supplied advice and counsel for the state efforts and provided the "battle plan" described above. It also assisted in developing the various strategies by which the state constitutional strictures on church and state could be evaded. Another example of this group's service can be seen in its adroit use of propaganda. A carefully planned national effort was launched early in 1969 and another in 1972. The Conference's news agency prepared and distributed a series of releases which were carried not only by the wire services, news magazines, and principal dailies, but also found their way, via ecumenical overtones, into principal Protestant publications. The propaganda was cleverly written to make it appear that government subsidies to Catholic schools were inevitable because they made such good sense. It was just a matter of time.

These releases were wide-ranging in character, offering examples from all over the country, and portraying the plight of the parochial schools not as a church problem, but as a national problem which the American people must somehow manage to solve. All made the same basic points. The Catholic schools were hard up. If the financial squeeze continued they would be forced to close and dump their students on the public schools. The continuance of the parochial schools was important dollar-wise since they "save the public money." They can educate students more cheaply than the public schools. The sudden influx of these students into the public system would sharply increase its cost thus adding substantially to the taxpayer's burden. It would pay the state to provide a little aid for the Catholic schools in the teaching of secular subjects rather than have this disaster occur. These planted pieces popped up everywhere and were heard on television and radio as well — usually without rebuttal.

Any considered examination of the evidence makes clear that state aid confers on religious schools a solid and definitive benefit: it enables these schools to continue their program of sectarian indoctrination. What state aid meant to one Catholic high school has been told by Father John A. Thomas, principal of Cardinal Stritch High School, East Toledo. He stated flatly: "A state grant saved us this year."[9] The state grant of $33,850 was used to supplement teachers' salaries. Hope for continuance of the parochial school lay in the fact that state aid was scheduled for sharp increase in ensuing years.

The solid grant from tax funds was equally decisive for St. Raphael School, a Catholic institution in Bay Village, a suburb of

Cleveland. Forty-four thousand, six hundred and ninety-nine dollars were allocated to this school, a sum that made the difference between survival and closing. The largest allocation, $26,000 went for salaries of school personnel. The rest was expended for science, testing, television and administrative costs. St. Raphael's was opting for full state support.

How state aid helped the Cincinnati archdiocese is indicated by a remark of Father Harmon Kenning, assistant superintendent of archdiocesan schools. "These funds will just manage to keep us in business."

In most of the church schools the state money was being used to supplement the salaries of teachers. Up to $3,000 for each instructor could be provided from this source. The actual allocation for private schools in Ohio for fiscal 1970 was $18,274,400. Most of this west to church schools, about 90 per cent of which were Catholic. Cuyahoga County received the largest allocation of $2,631,789. Hamilton County received the next largest grant — $1,491,903. These amounts were expected to double in the succeeding years and to move on, eventually, to full support.

A typical situation is that of the Oak Hills School District, Cheviot, Ohio.[10] State aid in this district flows to six schools, all of them Catholic. Aid comes under two state programs — one the 1969 act providing basic support, principally teachers' salaries, and the other the 1967 act providing for auxiliary services. For the 1969-70 school year the six Catholic schools received $240,000 which was just double what they had received the preceding school year. The funds not used to pay teachers went for movie projectors, film strip projectors and film strips, transparencies for overhead projectors, tape recorders and tapes, listening posts, library books, supplementary textbooks and magnetic boards. In addition to these funds from the state, the church schools also received federal aid under two federal laws — the ESEA and the National Defense Education Act. The level of this aid was scheduled for a slight decline in fiscal 1970 in contrast with the rapidly burgeoning state aid. Public assistance for busing to parochial schools — about $7.5 million — statewide was provided in addition.

Commenting on the state aid reaching the Catholic schools, Msgr. William N. Novicky, Cleveland diocesan superintendent of schools, remarked: "It will give us a breathing spell."[11]

The facts are that in the states where it is provided the flow of government aid enables the Catholic schools to continue their program. Similar legislation is being sought in most of the other states. What the waning convictions of parishioners could no longer sustain, the government now undertakes to support. The long suffering taxpayers are called upon to add the cost of religious schools to the myriad burdens they already bear. And this shift is being achieved by some of the most devious political maneuvering ever witnessed on the American scene. As the experience of Pennsylvania and Ohio and also New York shows, once these subsidies commence they tend to increase rather than decrease. Once this door has been opened even a little, churchmen can be counted on to force it open to full subsidy.

NOTES

1. Doerr, Edd, *The Conspiracy That Failed*. Americans United, 1968
2. *Ibid.* p. 35
3. CHURCH & STATE, September, 1967
4. CHURCH & STATE, September, 1969
5. CHURCH & STATE, December, 1966
6. *Long Island Press*, July 10, 1969
7. Concurrence in *Abington v. Schempp*. 374 U.S. 203 (1963
8. *The Nation*. December 15, 1969
9. *Toledo Blade*. November 23, 1969
10. *Western Hills Press*. Cheviot, Ohio, September 25, 1969
11. Cleveland *Plain Dealer*. August 24, 1969

5. Defense Does It: Helping the Church in Higher Education

Federal aid to institutions of higher learning provided the first major breakthrough for the churches in the area of educational assistance. This form of aid began with the National Defense Education Act of 1958, a measure subsequently expanded and blended into the Higher Education Facilities Act of 1963.

"Defense" was the label on this particular package of aid. Church institutions were included among the beneficiaries of this legislation on the ground that the nation could not afford to overlook this facet of its potential strength. A total mobilization of educational resources was imperative, it was argued, if the Russian challenge to our military and economic supremacy were to be countered.

The commencement of federal aid to church institutions in the area of higher education rather than lower schools was not accidental. The defense appeal was obviously stronger at this level. But in addition there was a highly practical consideration. The Protestants who had no elementary schools to speak of had a substantial stake in higher education. Government aid to church schools at the elementary level could almost be called Catholic aid since 90 per cent of it would flow to that church. The picture in higher education was quite different, however, Protestants had phased out most of their elementary schools a century and a half before and had committed themselves to the public system. But they had

85

steadily enlarged their commitment to higher education. It could be expected, therefore, that Protestants would look more benignly upon aid to colleges than to lower schools. In programs of aid to higher education Protestants would draw their share.

There was another angle of the horse trading over this legislation that is worth mentioning. Federal aid to higher education was initially offered to the Catholics in exchange for their approval of a bill providing aid for public elementary schools only. The Catholics did not buy this. They were happy enough over federal aid to their colleges but were in no mood to settle for that alone.

Shortly after the National Defense Education Act was signed by President Eisenhower, the federal government began providing academic facilities for numerous church sponsored colleges and universities. Despite its name, the law actually had nothing to do with defense except possibly in the most vague and remote sense. Its name was no more than a public relations gimmick tied in with the post-Sputnik surge in educational concern. The label conveyed the notion that the aid to be provided would somehow strengthen the nation's defense program which the Russians' brilliant Sputnik achievement had rendered suspect. Defense was an objective difficult to oppose at that particular juncture. It was used as a lever to get action on federal aid to education with church schools included. The defense appeal was utilized by Msgr. Frederick G. Hochwalt, chief lobbyist for the United States Catholic Conference when he appeared in 1961 before the House Committee to testify on a proposed extension of NDEA. "Basic to our consideration of the National Defense Education Act," he declared, "is our belief that the Federal Government has an obligation to help identify and bring to fruition the full potential of every youth. Further, it is our belief that failure to do this will imperil not only the individual, but the nation and the free world."

The use of the defense appeal in getting the legislation passed is illustrated by the remarks of Representative Edith Green of Oregon, chairman of the committee which prepared and sponsored the Higher Education Facilities Act:

Mr. Speaker, it seems to me that if we did not today have

86

the private colleges we could not successfully compete with the Russians. In this country there are about 2,000 colleges. Of these 2,000, 703 are public, 1,300 are private, 303 Roman Catholic, 406 Protestant, and 6 Jewish. I do not think that we could win the race to the moon if we did not have the educational programs provided in these great private institutions.[1]

There were substantial benefits for church schools in the legislation. These benefits represent the price the sponsors felt they had to pay for the support of the Catholic bloc, a group that practically held veto power over such legislation. First, there were loans to students receivable through church-related colleges. As amended in 1961, the Act provided that for persons teaching in either public or parochial schools the loans could be canceled up to 50 per cent.

Then there were fellowships for graduate study which were receivable through church-related colleges; also centers and institutes which could be sponsored by church-related colleges and financed by the government; and, finally, federal loans to church schools to acquire equipment for the teaching of secular courses. Twelve per cent of the funds were reserved for private schools, nearly all of which were church-related.

In 1961, the proposed NDEA extension became involved with President Kennedy's aid to education bill in a hassle with sectarian interests. Promoters of federal aid to church schools sought to obtain wider concessions in NDEA as a price for supporting President Kennedy's elementary and secondary school aid bill which did not include church schools at all. We have seen how after a good many offers and counter-offers the sectarian protagonists proclaimed themselves dissatisfied with the concessions they had won and used their control of the House Rules Committee to keep the education bill from coming to a vote. It died in that committee.

Meanwhile, the NDEA programs of aid for church schools were being extended and widened. Throughout the hearings on these bills there repeatedly appeared the assumption that the aid offered for loans to strengthen the teaching of science, matehmatics and modern foreign languages could not possibly involve aid to

87

religion. Of course, the aid went to the school in which religion was prominently taught and in which religious exercises and studies were compulsory for all students. But the committees stuck rigidly to the compartmental approach. Science and religion, for example, were two different things. If the school were paid for its science teaching program this could not possibly involve aid to religion.

Here we encounter that purposeful lack of imagination which steadily characterized the hearings and deliberations of the educational committees. One could as effectively argue that churches could be repaired at government expense because brick, mortar and timber are not religious — or that there could be no violation in the purchase of church pews because the wood in them was not religious. On at least one occasion Rep. Roman C. Pucinski, a ranking member of the House Committee, did express doubts about the possible religious content in the humanities, but he and his colleagues manifested throughout an unshaken assumption that there could be no possible religious emphasis or coloration in the subjects covered by NDEA. Dr. George R. LaNoue undertook to demonstrate the fallacy of this assumption by showing that in a parochial school such a division of curriculum into secular and religious did not occur.[2] What took place was not isolation of secular from religious but rather the permeation of secular with religious.

In establishing this thesis Dr. LaNoue performed an analysis of over 100 textbooks currently in use in church schools for the teaching of science, mathematics and languages. The schools were those of the Seventh-day Adventist Church, Christian Reformed, Missouri Synod Lutheran, and Roman Catholic. What ensued was a fascinating study bristling with photostatic reproductions which neatly demonstrated that church schools did indeed permeate even these nonreligious subjects with religion. As LaNoue put it:

> 'I have no objection to the presentation of these subjects in a specifically religious context. I merely wish to show that, contrary to the assumptions behind the National Defense Education Act, sectarian material has been integrated into the teaching of science, mathematics and languages in parochial schools. Religious doctrine can be taught in an algebraic formula or, at least, in an arithmetic book.[3]

The response of Congress to this incontrovertible evidence was peculiar. Instead of tightening up the aid programs at the point of the church schools, it actually widened the categories for which aid could be given.

Another rationale for federal aid to church-related colleges was that in the realm of higher education the church-state problem was somehow different from that of lower schools. This was the argument of President Kennedy who had stood firmly against any church school aid at the elementary and secondary level, but favored aid at the college level. At a news conference June 27, 1962, he explained it this way:

> I stated at that time (last year) that the briefs indicated, and my own analysis indicated, that there was not a comparable constitutional question on aid to higher education in nonstate colleges or universities.
>
> In my opinion, there are very clear limitations based on the Supreme Court decisions on aid to nonpublic schools in the secondary field. But in those fields the attendance is compulsory; it is universal.
>
> There is a particular tradition connected with our public school system which has placed it in a special place in the traditional and constitutional life of our country.
>
> This is not true of higher education. . . .[4]

How remote the NDEA was from defense is demonstrated by the fact that its fellowship grants were presently being employed for the training of the clergy. When this writer appeared before a Senate committee studying extension of NDEA on May 13, 1961, he pointed out that scores of fellowships had been granted under the Act for religious studies of seminarians.[5] The writer cited five fellowships granted to students in Union Theological Seminary, New York City, and three fellowships in Biblical studies to Emory University, and Duke University, both Methodist institutions. There were also fellowships for religious studies at Claremont College (originally United Church of Christ), Dropsie College, a Jewish institution, and the school of religion at Brown University (Baptist oriented). The writer asked the committee: "How can there be separation of church and state in a country where the government pays for the training of the clergy?"

In November, 1960, the Office of Education announced that it had allocated $6,480,000 in loans to private and parochial schools for equipment and remodeling and improving of facilities for teaching the secular subjects of science, mathematics and modern foreign languages. About 90 per cent of these funds went to Catholic institutions, but some Protestant and Jewish schools also benefited.

With the passage of the Higher Education Facilities Act of 1963, direct grants began to flow to church-related colleges. The original bill provided $1.2 billion in grants and loans over a three year period for 2,100 colleges and universities, 842 of which were church-related. The grants have been steadily widened and expanded ever since. A typical report published by the Office of Education in September, 1966 showed that 43 church-related colleges had received $14,953,218 during the latter part of fiscal 1966. The funds were allotted to 24 Roman Catholic colleges, five Lutheran, four Methodist, three Presbyterian, two Baptist, one each of Evangelical and Reformed, Assemblies of God, Disciples of Christ and Church of the Brethren, and one unidentified. More than $1.6 billion has been granted for college construction under the Act. Many a feeble church institution of higher learning got its start and momentum by construction grants of the Federal Government. Consider the case of Anderson College, an institution of the Church of God in Anderson, Indiana. This school received a grant of $1,076,251 for construction of an academic building, a start on its proposed $20 million campus. By the time this campus is completed one can be sure that most of it will have been built with federal funds. The Protestant Oral Roberts University of Tulsa, Oklahoma is another case in point.

Marymount College, a Roman Catholic school in Boca Raton, Florida, was literally put into business with federal aid. Marymount was founded in 1963. But before 1968 had passed this school had managed to wangle $2 million from the Federal Government for construction of dormitories. It also got a $55,000 OEO grant for a study of migrant children and another $10,000 education grant to promote adult women's education.

Have a look at the impact of federal aid on the Roman Catholic college in a single area — that of Buffalo, N.Y. Here are the grants of the Office of Education for one program only — that of Educational Opportunity — for 1970-71: Canisius $82,400; D'Youville $27,400; Niagara $43,300; Rosary Hill $56,300; St. Bonaventure $42,800.

The real significance of the federal aid to religious institutions is to be observed in the grants made to smaller schools. These federal grants either put the school into operation or kept it in operation when, without the aid, it would have expired. Take the case of an old Roman Catholic school, Mt. Angel College in Oregon, whose historic role has been the training of religious for the church. Plagued with financial problems, this little school received in 1970 a grant of $60,000 from the United States Office of Education which reportedly enabled it to complete the 1969-70 academic year. It is a safe surmise that Mt. Angel will now become a permanent dependent of the federal government.

Some of the federal grants are in the form of scholarship aid to the student. Some small church-related colleges are able to finance tuition for a considerable portion of their student body through these programs. Consider the substantial impact of the following educational opportunity grants announced by Rep. Joseph P. Vigorito for schools in his 24th Congressional District in Pennsylvania:

School	No. of Students	No. Students Aided	Religious Affiliation	Amount
Allegheny	1,150	107	Methodist	$58,900
Thiel	753	160	Lutheran	87,800
Gannon	2,306	371	Roman Catholic	204,000
Mercyhurst	589	223	Roman Catholic	27,600
Villa Maria	738	59	Roman Catholic	32,700

Consider the case of little Seton Hill and St. Vincent College in Pennsylvania, a Roman Catholic school which in the summer 1969 issue of its "Information Sheet" announced grants from various federal programs of $151,277. This comprised a substantial part of

91

the school's total budget. The cumulative effect of federal aid can be observed in the case of Carroll College, also Roman Catholic, of Helena, Montana. In 1968, Carroll got government grants and loans for a large academic building. Then in 1970, Carroll got a $50,000 grant to carry on an educational program in the building.

All such grants pale before those announced for Georgetown University of Washington, D.C., a school belonging to the Society of Jesus, which has a long record of government largesse. On April 26, 1970, it was announced that this institution would receive a federal grant of more than $8.5 million. The grant was to provide for expansion of the university's School of Medicine and would be made available over a four year period.

There are more than 150 different programs of federal aid to higher institutions of learning and the churches share in most of them. Other federal dispensing agents such as the OEO also give aid to church-related educational institutions. In addition to the federal programs, a growing number of states now provide their own forms of aid to church-related colleges. New York, California, Wisconsin, Missouri, Texas, Kansas, Georgia, Virginia and Tennessee have tuition grant programs under which the state pays to the qualifying student or, more properly to the school he has entered, a grant applicable to his tuition. What typically happens in these cases is that as soon as the legislature approved the program and sets it up, the college raises its tuition by the amount of the grant. Thus, the student is no better off, but the school benefits.

The report of the Wisconsin program is of interest. Since the grants are receivable only in colleges charging $400 or more tuition, none can go to students attending public colleges. During the first three years of this program (1965-1968) over 8,000 grants were made. The report shows that students at Catholic colleges received 61 per cent of all grants. Students at Protestant colleges received 14 per cent, while students in nonsectarian private colleges received 25 per cent. Two and one-third million dollars was spent on the program.

The California State Scholarship Program in the typical academic year of 1967-68 awarded $5.9 million in scholarship grants to 7,422 students. The scholarships averaged about $800 each. The

California program differs from the New York program in that competitive examinations are held and awards are made on the basis of merit. Students in church-related and other private colleges received 60 per cent of the scholarships and 88 per cent of the money even though they comprise but 11 per cent of the state's college population. These schools draw most of the funds because the money can go only for tuition and fees and the church-related colleges have the high tuition. Nineteen Protestant colleges, 18 Catholic colleges and 26 private nonsectarians drew an average $1,200 per year compared with $120 for public universities.

The Higher Education Facilities Act contains a sectarian disclaimer designed to protect it from challenge on First Amendment grounds. The law provides that federal funds may not be used for construction of a divinity school or facilities for religious instruction or worship, and that any government financed building may not be used for such purposes for a period of 20 years. As we shall see, this stipulation was eventually struck down by the Supreme Court which insisted that the ban on such programs in federally financed buildings must be permanent. While there was never any systematic surveillance of facilities or any real effort to enforce this provision, it did result in some embarrassing episodes. Typical of these problems is that posed by Ohio Valley College, a small denominational institution of Parkersburg, W.Va. This school built an auditorium with federal funds and was using the room for chapel services. A federal agent happened to walk in on one of these services. Since this was an obvious violation, he reported it. The school was thus placed in an embarrassing position. Its officials announced that they would endeavor to raise the funds and repay the government so that they might continue to use the facility for religious purposes.

There are a number of questions raised by the program of subsidies to church-related colleges. Does the ban on acts respecting establishment of religion cover financial grants to church-related colleges? If so, just what constitutes such an institution? Some colleges were originally started by churches but have grown away from their control and today have only nominal ties with their parent bodies. Are these to be included as church-related institutions? Or, should some account be taken of the current status?

93

Such issues cried for adjudication in the court but, as we shall have occasion to note, litigation by taxpayers had been rendered all but impossible. Congressional leaders wanted no court tests on the church-state issue for obvious reasons. Church-state separationists finally hit on a device for testing the issue in the Higher Education Facilities Act. For a long time the State of Maryland had been making grants to private colleges for construction purposes — exactly the sort of thing that was being done under the HEFA. There was no bar to taxpayer suits in the Court of Maryland. Why not, therefore, challenge the Maryland grants as in violation of the First Amendment in the likelihood that the case would be appealed to the United States Supreme Court? If the High Court were to strike down such grants by the State of Maryland the ban would also extend to the same kind of grants being made under federal laws.

Accordingly, the Horace Mann League, Americans United, and other groups, together with many Maryland taxpayers, challenged grants by the state ranging from $500,000 to $750,000 to Western Maryland (Methodist), Hood (United Church of Christ) and Notre Dame of Maryland and St. Joseph's (both Roman Catholic).[6] In a split decision the Maryland Court of Appeals struck down as in violation of the First Amendment the grants to the Methodist and Catholic colleges. In a decision almost as significant, the court upheld the grant to Hood College on the ground that its relation to the United Church of Christ was largely nominal and vestigial.

The decision in the Horace Mann case appeared, therefore, to turn on the relationship between the college and its sponsoring church. Where that relationship is definitive and controlling, then the college comes under the no-establishment law and, as a religious institution, may not receive tax support. But where the relationship is only nominal and not controlling, there is no church-state issue involved. Regarding the three institutions, the Maryland Court of Appeals held that:

> The operative effect of the bills . . . demonstrates in a legal and constitutional sense, a purpose to use the State's coercive power to aid religion; that the grants, if made, would constitute a contribution by the State of tax-raised funds to support institutions which teach the tenets and faith of a particular church; and

94

that the taxes levied to raise funds for the grants would be levied to help support religious activities and religious institutions.[7]

The majority opinion in Horace Mann written by Chief Judge Prescott contains a classic account of the wars, persecutions and other disruptions which have risen during the course of history from the intrusion of the state's coercive power into the realm of religion. But from a practical standpoint perhaps the most significant part of the opinion is the criteria set forth by the court for the purpose of determining what is and what is not a church-related college. There are, said the court, six criteria: (1) the stated purpose of the college; (2) the college personnel which includes the governing board, the administrative officers, the faculty and the student body (with considerable stress being laid on the substantiality of religious control over the governing board); (3) the college's relationship with religious organizations and groups, including the extent of ownership, financial assistance, the college's memberships and affiliations; (4) the place of religion in the college's program which includes the extent of religious manifestations in the physical surroundings, the character and extent of religious observances sponsored or encouraged by the college, the required participation of any or all students, the extent to which the college sponsors or encourages religious activity different from that of the college's own church and the place of religion in the curriculum and extra-curricular programs; (5) the result or "outcome" of the college program, such as accreditation and the nature and character of the activities of the alumni; and (6) the work and image of the college in the community.

The decision of the Maryland Court of Appeals set the stage for a climactic showdown in the United States Supreme Court. This did not come about for a long time. Even as the Horace Mann plaintiffs were girding for the Supreme Court test, that test was denied them. For reasons that will perhaps forever remain obscure the Court refused to take the case. Seldom has such a refusal created so tragic a wake of contradiction and confusion. The Court did not upset the Maryland ruling which said that grants by the State of Maryland to denominational colleges for construction violated the First

95

Amendment and the Fourteenth, which makes binding on the states all federal constitutional strictures. Nor did the Court examine and affirm the Maryland opinion.

Even when the Supreme Court did finally take a case involving federal aid to church related colleges (Tilton v. Richardson), the ruling by a badly divided Court lacked the precision and clarity that were needed. The decision which came down June 28, 1971 is analyzed in Chapter 6. In brief, the Court did let the federal grants stand because plaintiffs failed to show that the recipient institutions were specifically religious.

Where do we now stand on the issue of government subsidy of church-related colleges? The answer may be different in different situations. Certainly, the farther the school moves from a distinctly religious emphasis the more likely it will be to pass muster for federal aid.

In general the Court took the view that the indoctrination program was far less intense at the collegiate level than in elementary and secondary schools. Church-related colleges are apt to take a rather broad and general view of religion in teaching provided at this level, and to be more relaxed in the whole matter. This substantially reduces the problem of "entanglement" and lessens the danger of trespass on the First Amendment religion guarantees.

Thus, while the Court let the four grants in question stand, its language demonstrates that blanket grants for authentically church-related colleges with a religious mission are definitely not permissible. *Tilton* will not be the end of litigation on this issue.

Tilton did not really set aside Judge Prescott's opinion in *Horace Mann*. In a way it underscored this opinion for it reiterated that authentically sectarian institutions of higher learning could not draw government subsidies. While *Tilton* did not actually strike any grants, it had the effect of underscoring the criteria for discerning sectarianismm in colleges which *Horace Mann* had enunciated. What happened then was that the religious colleges, anxious about their budgets and clutching for every possible dollar, took *Horace Mann* more seriously than the Office of Education did. These institutions, in effect, started to conform to the *Horace Mann* criteria. The indecisive opinion in *Tilton* has accelerated this process. That is, in order to assure the continuance of state and federal aid, the administrators commenced, at least nominally, to divest their schools of religious control and religious teaching. A reading of the criteria established by Judge Prescott clearly shows that the more effectively a religious college pursues its religious purposes the less likely it is to pass muster on the no-establishment clause for federal or state aid. Many administrators seemed to believe that their choice was, therefore, between maintaining religion on campus and maintaining their very exitence. It seemed clear to them that their own sponsoring churches would be unwilling to provide adequate support and that it would be better to divest themselves of religion for the sake of government aid.

Not all colleges decided the issue this way. A number refused all federal aid and clung to their religious distinctives, but most began to go the other way. Lewis and Clark College of Portland, Oregon, was one of the first to sever its ties with its sponsor church, the United Presbyterian, and its principal motivation was the fear of losing government aid. Kentucky Southern College of Louisville, Kentucky, severed its relations with the Baptist Convention in order to receive federal aid as did the Baylor Medical School. Many denominational colleges are following suit today as their donations decline and government aid becomes increasingly necessary to their survival. Webster College, a small Catholic college near St. Louis, was taken out of the denomination and turned over to lay control by Sister Jacqueline Grennan. Though only a small school with 1,000 students, Webster had consistently been drawing a large part of its budget from the federal government. Its annual subsidy had been running about $350,000. The school's president explained the change to lay control on the ground that "higher education today is big business and it is becoming more difficult for a religious order to finance a college adequately from internal resources."[8]

Dilemma of the Church-Related College

The problem faced by the college administrators is that of de-religionizing their curriculum and campus sufficiently to draw government aid without alienating those who support the school precisely because it is denominational. There may be complaints from the latter if the institution overdoes its secularizing. So Patrick F.

Scanlan writes in the *Brooklyn Tablet:*

> It would appear to us that when a Catholic institution loses its religious character it not only betrays its founders and its ideals but it defrauds the parents of its students. All the amount of grandstanding . . . attachment to Ivy League institutions or misinterpretations of ecumenism does not excuse secularization. . . . Parents in the course of a brief time will no longer be paying four and five times the cost of education in a Catholic-named college if it is little different than a public institution.[9]

Consider, too, the protest of the Rev. Marvin R. O'Connell in *The Catholic News,* March 26, 1970. Insisting that theology should be a required study for all students at a Catholic college, he asked: "Otherwise, how can we justify the vast expenditure involved? If there is nothing intellectually . . . distinctive about the Catholic college, why keep it open?"

The dilemma of the church-related college as posed by federal aid can be clearly seen in the testimony offered in the Horace Mann case. When we place the testimony of the administrators alongside the devout affirmations of the college catalogues there is an interesting contrast. The audiences were, of course, different. The testimony was for the benefit of justices who were to decide if grants by the State of Maryland were in violation of the First Amendment. The catalogues were for parents seeking a college with a religious atmosphere for their children.

Hood College, for example, stressed in its catalogue that it was church-related and emphasized its compulsory chapel services. "The ideals of high academic achievement and of religious commitment are complementary, and both are necessary to complete education. . . ," the college bulletin declared. But when Hood's president, Dr. Randle Elliott went on the stand to defend his school's right to public funds, he took a different line. He declared there was such freedom at his school that a professor could teach that Jesus was not divine, or that there is no life hereafter. If the church tried to interfere with his school, he said that he would ignore it.

The Western Maryland College stated unequivocally that this was a school of the Methodist Church; that it required attendance each Sunday at the college chapel service; and that the school "feels a responsibility to encourage spiritual interests." On the witness stand, however, Western Maryland president, Dr. Lowell S. Ensor, stated that it would be quite possible for a professor there to teach that he did not believe in the divinity of Christ or in his resurrection. Brigadier General Robert J. Gill (Retired) testified that he had been a trustee of Western Maryland for 39 years and that he had never known the Methodist Church to seek to influence the college in any way.

Perhaps the crux of the trial came in questions pertaining to possible appointment of an atheist to the faculty. Three of the colleges could not quite take that one. The presidents of Western Maryland, Notre Dame of Maryland, and St. Joseph's all testified that they would not knowingly hire an atheist for their faculty. But the president of Hood stated that he would have no problem with this. The point was important since it involved a question of possible sectarian bias in the hiring policy of an institution supported with public funds. It is significant that the three institutions which stated they would not hire atheist faculty members lost their grants, while the one that was open to atheist faculty members kept its grant. There were, to be sure, many factors in the eventual decision, but this one certainly had its impact.

The Catholic problem in higher education has been even more severe at this point than the Protestant, since Catholic control of its institutions has tended to be more pervasive. The situation in New York provides an excellent example of the problems that rise when institutions under tight, sectarian control of this kind seek subsidy from a state where church-state constitutional provisions are strict. Under a New York law private colleges may receive grants based on the number of degrees conferred — $400 for each bachelor's and master's and $2,400 for each doctorate during a 12-month period. But the church-state provisions in the New York Constitution specifically bar the aid to any school "wholly or in part under the control or direction of any religious denomination." Hence, there was a program of inspection based largely on the Horace Mann criteria to determine whether the school was religious enough to be disqualified for state aid.

Eventually, twenty-one sectarian colleges were turned down, most of them Roman Catholic. The examiners paid particular attention to the institution's announced purposes and goals, the composition of its governing board, the content of its religion courses, and whether such courses were compulsory. Schools refused aid were Canisius, D'Youville, Iona, King's, Manhattanville, Marist, Marymount, Manhattan, Mount Saint Mary, Mount Saint Vincent, Nazareth, New Rochelle, Niagara, Notre Dame of Staten Island, Rosary Hill, St. Francis, St. Joseph's, St. Rose, St. Thomas Acquinas, Siena, and Wagner. Keuka College, a Baptist-founded school in Penn Yan was given $56,000 for the 1969-70 school year. The inspectors found "no vestigial remnants of religious control" at Keuka and added: "We don't feel this particular institution is under the Blaine Amendment. So far as we're concerned, it doesn't even have a nominal [religious] affiliation now."

The questionnaire sent out by the state because of Article XI, Section 3 was blasted by the Very Rev. William L. Reilly, S.J., president of LeMoyne College, who said that his school "did not deem it advisable to reply." He decried it as "against both logic and justice" and felt that aid should have been given to his school without any interrogation.

Consider, especially, the case of Fordham University, a Jesuit institution located in New York City. Under the New York law Forham could receive $1 million annually in operating funds from the state — provided it could qualify as nonsectarian. Fordham is one of 28 institutions of higher learning in the United States owned and operated by the Jesuit Order. Not too many years ago the governing boards of all these institutions, Fordham included, were composed solidly of Jesuit priests. For Fordham to receive funds of the State of New York appeared to be impossible.

But Fordham went to work on the problem. The university spent $45,000 on a study to see how the school would have to change in order to qualify for state aid. The study done by two professors from Columbia University, reported that the result could be accomplished by the school without, as they delicately put it, "changing itself so drastically that old friends would no longer know it." This study published in book form proves to be a fascinating presentation of just which images must come down, what prayers omitted, and what religious personnel and practices shifted in order to produce the requisite dereligionizing of the school. (See Walter Gellhorn and R. Kent Greenawalt, *The Sectarian College and the Public Purse*,

100

Oceana Publications, Dobbs Ferry, N.Y. 1970). It worked, too. As a result of the de-religionizing measures that were taken, Fordham was eventually approved by the State Education Commission for state aid under the Bundy Plan. The New York State Constitution being as it is, this simply meant the Commissioner had decided that Fordham was not a definitely Catholic or religious school. Also found to be qualified for state aid were two other Roman Catholic schools, Manhattanville College and St. John Fisher College. Commissioner Nyquist found "after an extensive and careful review that none (of these institutions) is now under the control and direction of a religious denomination or teaches denominational tenets or doctrine."

Classification of St. John Fisher College as secular for the purposes of state subsidy aroused the protest of a businessman, M.V. Little, who wrote indignantly to Frederick M. Binder, Associate Commissioner for Higher Education on March 11, 1970:

> How can you say that this institution is not now under the control of a religious denomination when the trustees are four "religious" and 3 lay people (presumably Roman Catholics) and whose chancellor is Roman Catholic Bishop Kearney? The Commission of Education must think that the people of this state are a pack of fools.

An on-the-spot investigation of St. John Fisher by Charles H. Sumner of Rochester, N.Y. for Americans United disclosed many interesting characteristics of denominational presence and control. He found religious symbols on every hand. One of the buildings is named St. Basil Hall. Another, named Becket Hall, serves as a residence for candidates for the priesthood. This building is actually owned by the Roman Catholic Diocese of Rochester and stands on land leased by the college. Another building is owned by the Basilian Fathers for their candidates for the priesthood and Basilian teachers. Inscriptions over the doors read: "St. Thomas Moore, pray for us," "St. Joseph, pray for us" and "Hail Mary, full of grace." The catalogue describes St. John Fisher as "a Catholic College of Arts and Sciences under the direction of the Basilian Fathers." The college shield has emblems which are described in such terms as "... honors the most blessed Trinity ... honoring

Mary as Queen of Heaven and Earth . . ." The academic year "commences with the Mass of the Holy Spirit . . . attended by the entire faculty and student body."

The president of St. John Fisher is a clergyman, the Rev. Charles J. Lavery and the dean is the Rev. Joseph B. Dorsey. The top floor of the administration building serves as residence for the priests who teach at the school. Chancellor of St. John Fisher is the diocesan bishop. Trustees are said to be four religious and three laymen. The catalogue (1968-1970) states that "the College endeavors to have its students achieve full and meaningful participation in the Masses." Twelve hours of theology are required. The Nocturnal Adoration Society is one of the extracurricular activities recommended. Mr. Sumner predicted that the new college catalogue shortly to appear would delete all sectarian references in order to depict the college as a secular institution that could unquestionably qualify for state aid. Sure enough, there were many changes. For example, the old version stated that Fisher was "a Catholic college under the direction of the Basilian Fathers." The new version notes that "in 1968 ownership and control of the college were assumed by an independent Board of Trustees which includes men of Protestant, Catholic and Jewish faiths who are leaders in the professional, business and academic communities, thus making St. John Fisher College a private and independent College of Arts, Science and Commerce." Mr. Sumner's new investigation disclosed the retention of many forms of denominational control, however.

Before long the denominational controversy got really complicated. Officials of Canisius College of Buffalo, a Roman Catholic school, were resentful because Fordham qualified as secular for purposes of state aid but Canisius was ruled too religious. They argued that they were just as secular as Fordham and went to court to prove it. Canisius hired as its counsel Charles S. Desmond, a retired chief justice of the New York Court of Appeals who, while sitting on the bench, had publicly advocated state subsidy for church institutions. Attorneys for Canisius said that no one could show them how Canisius was any more religious than Fordham. They noted that Canisius had ten laymen and six religious on its Board of Trustees while Fordham had fifteen laymen and thirteen religious. It seemed to them that Canisius had "done better" in that category. Thus was presented an anomaly: a church school filing suit to compel support by a state whose constitution completely and rigidly prohibits such support.

To compound the anomaly, Iona College, another Roman Catholic school, joined the suit. If this school were not to be supported by the state, the state would have to show it why.

Even the so-called convent schools of the Roman Catholic Church have been feeling these pressures for change. Something is at work here considerably more substantial than a vague desire for change, or a growing spirit of secularism. These institutions, too, are eager for government financing and are willing to shed at least the trappings of religion in order to get it. Fontbonne College of St. Louis, a school long operated by a religious order known as the Sisters of St. Joseph Carondelet, has moved to broaden its base of control. Early in 1970 it was announced that the school would henceforth be directed by a board of trustees a majority of whom would be laymen. The governing body is to have eighteen members. Eleven will be laymen and seven will be members of the St. Joseph's order. The announcement stressed, however, that "now, as in the past, the college will be guided by the spiritual and intellectual ideals of the Sisters of St. Joseph, who will be its core group."

The Catholic University of America, traditionally a pontifical school directed by the Vatican, has also sought to lessen this form of clerical control. (This school currently receives about 25 per cent of its budget from the federal government.) Under new rules that have been formulated, the 30-member board of trustees will be elected by a majority vote of the board itself. Members are to be equally divided between clergymen and laymen, though, curiously, nuns and brothers are classified as laymen. In the past, all cardinals heading dioceses in the United States were automatically members. The crucial point that has been left undetermined is the role of the chancellor, Cardinal O'Boyle, Archbishop of Washington, who has traditionally held responsibility for enforcing orthodoxy of doctrine at the Catholic University. This has been handled in the by-laws with deliberate vagueness since the matter was said to be under study at the Vatican. A statement issued by Brother Nivard Scheel, administrative vice president, denied that the changes would mean a secularization of the school. He told the *New York Times* Feb. 6, 1970, that the school "is no less Catholic than it was before."

The problems of disassociation from denominational control will prove formidable because of the very vigor of Catholic management in the past. Here is another instance. The pontifical institution, Catholic University of America, has a Program of Affiliation for Catholic colleges which provides important guidelines for their operation. These guidelines lay heavy emphasis on religion. We read repeatedly of the basic importance of Catholic indoctrination to the program of the school.

> As Catholic educators (we) are concerned primarily with the development and maturation of today's youth for Christian living, based on Christian values and certain absolutes and moral standards. . . .
>
> We ourselves must be firmly and thoroughly grounded in our own philosophy of education. . . . This philosophy must be carefully and fully stated and accepted by all those working toward the common goals of Catholic education. It must permeate every aspect of the education process if it is to permeate the product of that process.

Again, we read from this "Program of Affiliation:"

> A Catholic philosophy of life is centered around certain fundamental truths, absolute and unchanging: man's origin and eternal destiny; his true nature, as a fallen being redeemed by Jesus Christ; his dependence on God and his relationship to Him and to the created universe; the dignity of the human being as a child of God, the brotherhood of man, and the responsibilities of justice and charity which follow therefrom. . . .
>
> . . . our educational subject is to be the "whole man" and our aim is to form the "true Christian."

It is worth noting, too, that the samples of curricula offered in connection with proposed departments of concentration regularly feature courses in religion.

It seems evident that the Program of Affiliation of the Catholic University will have to be subjected to the same process of de-religionizing as we have observed on the campuses of the church-related colleges.

The reception of tax dollars collected under coercion from all citizens into a sectarian institution whose tenets are accepted by only a fraction of them, is bound to affect the religious emphasis on such a campus. Such an emphasis will inevitably be diluted. Once these funds enter, the faculty is, in effect, required to play down and minimize the very purpose for which the institution was established. This is not to say that religion is barred from the campus. Not at all: what is barred is sectarian religion. What is barred is the dynamic of religion, the cutting edge of religion. The school can teach about religion but it may not indoctrinate. What is indicated is a polite, stand offish treatment of the subject. The faculty will teach the Bible in the same way as they would teach the Upanishads or the Koran. The administration must see to it that the prayers uttered on the campus must not get to anyone but must be, rather, in the nature of sterile exhibitions. What is to be sought is not engagement in religion, but an at-arms-length, carefully guarded display of the thing; not an experience of religion but an objective perusal of it.

What occurs is a de facto subversion of the religious emphasis in the religious school. As Dr. Paul Reynolds of Wesleyan University has pointed out — in all other subjects, save only this, what is sought is performance. The idea is to get the students to *do* mathematics and physics; to *re-live* and *make* history; to *become* statesmen and businessmen; to *write* poetry; *paint* pictures; *out-think* Plato. But now on the campus of the church-related college supported with public funds the idea is to water the thing down and make it sufficiently sterile to pass the test.

There is a simple and obvious consequence of federal aid to a church-related institution which is commonly overlooked or ignored. What happens when the tax dollars flow into such a school is that the full spectrum of civil rights comes with them. Perhaps the first impact of this is felt in the matter of admissions. The idea of a college serving its own denominational group is immediately laid to rest. For it would be unthinkable that there should be a religious test as to admissions in a school supported with tax funds. But there are other effects quite as decisive. Hope College, an institution of the Reformed Church in America, had for many years a requirement for attendance at chapel services. Some students did not care to go and got the American Civil Liberties Union to intervene on their behalf. A nice point was raised: could persons be compelled to attend religious services on the campus of a school subsidized with federal grants? The school dropped compulsory chapel.

Fairfield College, a Roman Catholic school of Fairfield, Conn., was one of the successful defendants in *Tilton v. Richardson*. That is to say, the school kept its federal construction grant when the Supreme Court ruled it was not definitely sectarian. The practical effect of the decision was manifested in an episode which took place shortly afterward.

According to the *Catholic Standard*, Dec. 23, 1971, Dr. Joseph Caffrey, a former Jesuit priest turned agnostic, was fired. An agnostic theology teacher did not seem appropriate at a Catholic school. But Dr. Caffrey, a resourceful man, pointed out that Fairfield's President, Father William McInnes, had testified in the *Tilton* case that his school had no religious test for faculty members. As soon as the point was made, Father McInnes withdrew the pink slip and reinstalled Dr. Caffrey. There can be no religious test for faculty in a school receiving federal aid!

Agnes Scott, a Presbyterian college in Georgia, had a challenge to its hiring policies. The school had a rule that only Christians could be hired for its faculty, hardly an unreasonable requirement for a Christian school. But when Jews learned of it they publicly protested and charged discrimination. Agnes Scott had neither sought nor received federal grants. Had it done so, the rule requiring Christians only for the faculty would have had to be dropped at once. An institution supported with public funds would not be permitted a religious test for faculty hiring. It would have to hire qualified persons regardless of their religion or lack of it.

Then there is the whole realm of labor relations. On June 15, 1970, the National Labor Relations Board announced that it would assume jurisdiction over labor problems in private colleges. Schools that have received federal aid will naturally have top priority here. This simply means that a labor dispute in such a school will bring in the National Labor Relations Board to take charge and make the arrangements. Where the federal money is the federal controls will inevitably follow.

What can we conclude? Certainly that federal aid to church institutions of higher learning has dealt a blow to separation of church and state in the field of education. By its early refusal to incorporate provisions for a court test on the church-state issue, Congress has been able to get a program of dubious constitutionality going with years of precedent and a flow of billions of tax dollars to church institutions. But there are other effects almost equally significant. The federal aid program has led to a nominal withdrawal of the churches from management of their institutions, at least to the degree necessary to obtain government financing. It has placed clerics in the difficult position of surrendering nominal control while seeking to retain de facto control.

As to religious emphasis on the campus, the effect of federal aid has been decisive. Such emphasis has been steadily diluted and weakened. It may be that the time has come to ask whether there remains any legitimate role for the church in the realm of general higher education. Is the church-related college merely another educational arm of the state, performing, a bit more feebly perhaps, a service which the state itself already performs? Is it the task of the church to train engineers, lawyers, teachers, doctors, dentists and nuclear physicists? If so, how does its function here differ from that of the state institution? These questions have never really been faced, let alone answered.

There is another problem: the ambivalence of the church's role in a quasi public institution. It appears evident that the campus of the traditional church-related college is rapidly becoming as secularized as that of its public counterpart, the state university. What is left is the shadow of religious control without the substance of religious teaching and practice.

Dr. Raymond W. Miller, longtime trustee of two church-related institutions — American University of Washington, D.C. and Pacific University of Oregon — has proposed a resolution of this ambivalence. He has urged that such institutions sever their church relationship because "college and university education today has gone beyond the financial and administrative power of the church to handle."[10] This would release church funds for the seminaries where the clergy are trained, and possibly for a few institutions that would be definitely church-related. Dr. Miller uses the analogy of the church academies which at one time handled most of the secondary education in the United States. He notes that "eventually the costs of operation became so great, and competition with public schools so keen, that most of them were abandoned. . . . A comparable change is now due at the level of higher education."

Dr. Miller's proposal points up the choice before the church-related college today. It can "go public," practically speaking, as a result of developments brought about by the receipt of public funds. In this situation the clergy and their associates may seek by various devices to retain control while ostensibly surrendering it for the sake of public subsidy. Such an ambivalence in a school will not do much either for education or religion.

But there is another choice. The forthright recommendation of Dr. Miller gains force and credence:

> Since the (church-related) institution is already in its general shape and posture a public institution, I believe it should become so in actual ownership, direction and financing. The church could thus concentrate in those areas that lie within the field of religious education and also increase its help to its seminaries.[11]

Notes

1. *Congressional Record.* September 20, 1962

2. *Phi Delta Kappan.* June, 1962

3. Ibid.

4. *Washington Post.* June 28, 1962

5. *Federal Aid to Parochial Schools.* Americans United, 1961, p.37

6. *Horace Mann v. Maryland Board of Public Works.* No. 356, Sept. Term, 1965— filed June 2, 1966

7. Ibid.

8. CHURCH & STATE, March, 1967

9. *Brooklyn Tablet.* March 7, 1968

10. CHURCH & STATE, May, 1969

11. Ibid.

6. Is the End Run Constitutional? Church and State in the Courts

We have to contemplate the indubitable fact that both federal and state subsidies have been flowing to church institutions, notably in the field of education. They are not flowing altogether freely but they are flowing. We are faced at once with two questions. First, is it wise socially and politically to subsidize selective schools like those of the church? Second, is such a procedure constitutional? There is constant talk of helping children but the only children who can be helped in private church schools are those granted admission to them. Admission to these institutions is severely restricted in a variety of ways. First, on the basis of religion. Sectarian schools exist to serve a particular religious clientele and even if they would be permitted to enroll, those of other faiths would be reluctant to do so. Then, second, these schools are *de facto* racially segregated since the percentage of blacks in them is far less than in the public schools (4.8 per cent compared with 14.5 per cent). Because of this fact the church schools may be said to contribute to racial imbalance in the schools. Again, there is selectivity at the point of aptitude. These schools often give admission tests and choose the most gifted. There is selectivity on the basis of behavior, since the church schools automatically eliminate all delinquents and problem cases by sending them into the public system. Finally, there is economic selectivity. Only those are admitted who, by one means or another, can pay the fees. The fees will undoubtedly persist whether or not the institutions receive public subsidy, and if tuition grants are paid by the state the tuition charges will inevitably rise.

It is a question of social policy whether the public is to subsidize schools which have the privilege of skimming off the best students for themselves and leaving the rest. If we had no constitutional tradition whatever in such matters, would this be sound practice?

Also involved in the issue of public subsidy to church schools are matters of public policy. Church teaching and public policy do not always coincide; as a matter of fact, they are sometimes contradictory. Birth control is an example. It is the policy of government in the United States to provide birth control clinics and to assist parents in the problem of intelligent limitation of the size of their families. But it is the official position of the Catholic Church as expressed in the 1968 papal encyclical *Humanae Vitae* that all recourse to artificial birth control is sinful and wrong.

On October 11, 1968 Cardinal O'Boyle summoned 1,500 parochial school teachers of his Washington, D.C. archdiocese and indoctrinated them in the kind of anti-birth control teaching to be promulgated in his denominational schools. He was doing what seemed perfectly logical to him. The schools exist for sectarian purposes and that is how he was using them.

Yet public policy in the United States today points in exactly the opposite direction. What sense does it make to subsidize with public funds sectarian schools whose teachings contradict public policy? Such teaching is properly tolerated as a matter of religious freedom, but to subsidize it with public funds would be the height of folly.

Apart from the social issue, though related to it, is the constitutional question. "Congress shall make no law respecting an establishment of religion. . . ." How does this provision, now applicable to the states as well, bear upon the matter of public subsidy for church institutions? How will the Supreme Court view this matter? Will it hold, as it has so often asserted, that what may not be done directly may not be done indirectly? Or will the Court buy child benefit and the various other circumventions that have been devised, and eventually approve the subsidies?

Will the courts, and especially the Supreme Court, now countenance an egregious distortion of the First Amendment? The legislative politician is, as a rule, more susceptible to this sort of thing than the judge on the bench. As the legislator typically views it, his first

110

responsibility as a politician is to be elected to office. Having been elected, it then becomes his responsibility to be re-elected. Without this, he is nothing. Hence, he is the available target for every kind of legislative foolishness that any determined sector of the electorate may seek to impose. Judges, too, come in for a certain amount of this since, in the lower courts, they are frequently subject to popular election.

The higher judiciary is supposed to be free of bloc pressures, however. Its role in the check and balance of a constitutional government has been highly celebrated. It is the function of the justices to keep government on the constitutional track. If, due to some passing fad or passion, the legislative swings out of orbit, it is their role to bring it back. The question, therefore, is: what can be expected of the courts in this contest between constitutional provisions and the determined effort of a clerical clique to nullify them by circumvention? On the face of it, the answer would seem to be clear. The Supreme Court will continue to reaffirm the establishment clause in clear accents as it has in the past. After all, the Court has already found that an innocuous prayer repeated every morning in the schools of New York aided religion so substantially that it did constitute an "act respecting establishment" and ordered the practice terminated. What then of the billions of dollars in prospect for church schools? If the prayer is establishment, can the billions be less so?

The logic of this appears impeccable, but the outcome is by no means as certain as it seems to indicate. It is often alleged that the Supreme Court is not so susceptible to political pressures as elected officials. But this does not mean the Court can be counted on for strict construction of the Constitution. The justices are sometimes swayed from such a course if they detect a social consensus moving in another direction. If the justices suspect that there is a massive shift in public opinion away from church-state separation and toward a permissiveness on public financing of church institutions, some of them will begin to look favorably upon the legal fictions constructed by clever lawyers to rationalize it. Had not the separate but equal doctrine stood virtually unquestioned for a century before the Court struck it down in the *Brown* case in 1954? The Court rather abruptly decided that separate though equal schools for blacks by the bare fact of segregation did impair their constitutional rights. This was a decision in the light of what the Court took to be a shifting social consensus.

We are moving here in an ephemeral and nebulous realm. It is not properly a realm of law at all but rather a realm of feeling and instinct. It is possible for the Court to be brilliantly right when it acts in the light of such considerations. On the other hand, it can miss the ball tragically. Under the intent of ushering in a new day, it can bring back an old night.

Should the hinted metamorphosis occur, we shall have witnessed a remaking of the law by the courts with scant regard for the total democratic process and, utlimately, a disdain for the people. The courts — and one must say preeminently the Supreme Court — would be yielding to a vociferous and clamant pressure group in a manner destined to become increasingly unacceptable to the great majority of the American people. The Court would be adding sectarian strife and anticlericalism to the other forms of divisiveness which plague the nation. As we shall see, the Supreme Court has not done this. But separationists now know they cannot count on the Court alone. They must battle in the political arena as well. They must win the mind of the people.

What has been the history of Supreme Court decisions on the crucial issue of government subsidy to church institutions? The Court had never met the issue head-on because, prior to the 1960s, no direct grants to sectarian institutions and programs had ever been made. The *Everson* case of 1947, mentioned in Chapter 2, approached the issue from an oblique angle. A New Jersey community was giving a rebate to children on bus tickets purchased for conveyance to school. These rebates had been extended to children attending a Catholic parochial school. Did this extension of the rebate for transportation to students in a church school constitute an act respecting establishment of religion?

By the narrowest possible margin, 5 to 4, the Supreme Court held that this program did not trespass upon the First Amendment. It did not trespass because the form of aid given was held to be no more than a safety measure which had nothing at all to do with the educational program of the school. Though the Court held the school aid issue was not actually involved in the suit, it did deal with

112

that matter, nevertheless. It was as though the Court were going out of its way to anticipate the money issue and to state its doctrine of the First Amendment in regard to it. What Justice Black wrote in his majority opinion is worth repeating here:

> The "establishment of religion" clause of the First Amendment means at least this: Neither a state nor the federal government can set up a church. Neither can pass laws which aid one religion, aid all religions, or prefer one religion over another. Neither can force nor influence a person to go to or remain away from church against his will or force him to profess a belief or disbelief in any religion. . . . No tax in any amount, large or small, can be used to support any religious activities or institutions, whatever they may be called, or whatever form they may adopt to teach or practice religion.[1]

How can the direction of this be mistaken? The intent is not to reckon some circuitous means by which public funds could be diverted into church schools. Surely the intent is the opposite — to bar as tightly as language can bar it — the door against church school subsidies. As though saying this once were not enough, the Court has gone on saying it again and again. The identical language quoted above has been repeated by the Supreme Court majority in *McCollum v. Board of Education* (1948), *Zorach v. Clauson* (1952), *Torcaso v. Watkins* (1961), *McGowan v. Maryland* (1961), and *Schempp v. Abington* (1963). It may be that no single passage of any decision rendered by the Supreme Court of the United States has ever been repeated in as many opinions as this one. The purpose in reiteration was to nail the thing down, to make it more than clear that under the First Amendment church schools could not be sustained with government money.

In *McCollum v. Board of Education* plaintiffs challenged constitutionality of a public school program for the teaching of religion. Students were taught religion during a period of released time — a half hour for elementary students and 45 minutes for secondary students. The students were divided into three groups — Protestant, Catholic and Jewish — and instruction was provided for them in the public classrooms. (No Jewish instruction had been offered for several years prior to the suit.) The McCollum child on whose behalf the suit was brought was the only child whose parents chose not to have him participate. He was relegated to a room by himself and became the object of ridicule and abuse by fellow students.

The Court's opinion found that this plan represented

> . . . beyond all question a utilization of the tax-established and tax-supported public school system to aid religious groups to spread their faiths. And it falls squarely under the ban of the First Amendment (made applicable to the States by the Fourteenth) as we interpreted it in *Everson v. Board of Education.*[2]

One can see in the following the "money line" doctrine of the First Amendment. It was not alone the promotional and organizational expertise of the public school system that served the cause of religion. It was also the money power which paid the teachers who administered the program, and also provided, furnished, and heated the rooms that were used.

> . . . . Here not only are state's tax-supported public school buildings used for the dissemination of religious doctrines. The State also affords sectarian groups an invaluable aid in that it helps to provide pupils for their religious classes through use of the State's compulsory public school machinery. This is not separation of Church and State.[3]

The New York case of *Zorach v. Clauson* (1952) was, again, not a church school subsidy case as such. As in *McCollum,* it was a case involving released time for religious instruction. The principal difference was that in *Zorach* the students were simply dismissed at the request of their parents and left the school premises to receive religious instruction elsewhere. This arrangement the Court upheld in a split decision 6 to 3. But here again we encounter the money doctrine of both *Everson* and *McCollum:*

> Government may not finance religious groups nor blend secular and sectarian education nor use secular institutions to force one or some religion on any person. . . . But it can close its door or suspend its operations as to those who want to repair to their religious sanctuary for worship or instruction. No more than that is undertaken here.[4]

The cases involving prayer and Bible reading in the public schools also had profound implications for the money question. We

114

must recall that one of the rationales for the separate Catholic school system had been that the public schools were actually Protestant schools rife with religious observances and teaching of this persuasion. In the course of a hundred years virtually all of this religious coloration had been eliminated from the public schools save for the practices complained of in these cases (*Engel v. Vitale, Abington v. Schempp,* and *Murray v. Curlett.*) Such practices were the reading of a passage from the Bible and the repetition of a prayer, often in connection with the flag salute at the beginning of the school day.

The practices were brought under challenge as violations of the establishment clause of the First Amendment. The Court found for the plaintiffs in all three instances and directed the discontinuance of compulsory religious exercises in the schools. Who cannot see that had they held otherwise they would have had to shift their ground on public subsidies to church schools? If it is constitutional to assemble students under compulsory attendance laws and impose religious exercises on them, then where is the fault in providing some government aid for schools which exist for religious purposes?

The *Engel* case, for example, concerned a prayer which had been prepared under the direction of the New York State Board of Regents and made mandatory for all public school students. (After the suit was filed absence from the prayer was granted upon request.) The authorization of this prayer was challenged as in violation of the First and Fourteenth Amendments to the Federal Constitution. The Supreme Court agreed with the plaintiffs and ordered New York to drop the religious practice in its schools.

The money issue figured in all of the prayer and Bible reading cases. As Justice Douglas pointed out in his *Engel* concurrence, a part of the time of New York officials, however miniscule, had gone into the preparation of the Regents' Prayer and also in its daily promulgation in the schools.[5] Expenditure of taxpayer's money for such a purpose was a violation. Again, the inference is obvious: if the First Amendment were violated by the use of public funds for such apparently minor and trivial religious exercises, what would be said of public subsidies to schools which were founded and operated for basically religious considerations?

Today we are in the very midst of a period of crucial litigation on the church-state issues. Some would call it a time of agonizing reappraisal. Cases now in process of adjudication will determine the general course of church-state relations for as much as a century. Powerful protagonists seek to change the entire concept of separation at the money line. How are the advocates of church school subsidy pleading these cases? How are these persons going about the business of persuading the courts that "no law" does not really mean "no law" but rather some laws under certain conditions? It is almost incredible: they are undertaking it with the plea that the church schools are not really religious! The argument runs like this. It is true that church schools do have one course in religion, but it is small and inconsequential. Most of the curriculum is exactly the same as that of the public schools. Since the church schools educate children in accordance with the compulsory education laws of the state, they may receive funds of the state for the performance of this task. Therefore, with the exception of a minor class, religion, the entire cost of the school can be borne by the state without violating the ban on aid to sectarian schools.

The following quotations from the record of one of these cases, *Americans United v. Essex,* show how it was pleaded by the diocesan intervenor as party defendant.[6] The questions by David J. Young, attorney for the diocese, and the answers by Father George A. Fulcher, pastor of St. Anthony's Catholic School:

Q. Do you have a school in connection with your church?
A. We do have a school. . . .
Q. Do the teachers at St. Anthony School attempt to teach the dogma of the Catholic Church in the required secular courses?
A. I am not aware of it in any instance. . .
Q. Do you try to make them do that?
A. No.
Q. Do you believe it would be educationally sound to do that?
A. I do not.

Carol Morris, a teacher at Our Lady of Victory, a Catholic school, answered Mr. Young as follows:

Q. Has any Bishop or other dignitary of the Catholic Church ever tried to persuade you to teach the dogma of the Catholic

116

faith when you are teaching your secular courses?

A. No, not at all.

Q. Has anyone ever tried to influence or coerce you to teach the dogma of the Catholic faith when you are teaching your math or science class?

A. No.

Sue Ann Fulton, a Methodist teaching at St. Paul's Catholic School, answered Mr. Young in this fashion:

Q. What grade do you teach?

A. I teach the Fourth Grade and I teach Eighth Grade reading.

Q. Do you teach the religious course in the Fourth Grade?

A. I do not. . . .

Q. During your six years at St. Paul's School has anyone ever asked you to teach religion in your secular courses that you teach?

A. No one has ever brought up the subject of religion to me in any way. . . .

Q. Do you think it would be educationally sound to try to teach religion in the required secular courses that you teach?

A. No, I do not. . . .

The impression carefully nurtured by Attorney David Young was of a purely secular school, largely staffed by non-Catholics, doing the same job as the public school — just educating children. All the religion the Catholic schools would admit to was a scant half-hour period. When asked why then, they insisted on separate, sectarian schools, since they were merely duplicating the public system, the teachers and administrators were in some difficulty. Protestant schoolmen frankly acknowledged the religious orientation of their schools, but Catholics adhered to the secular stance throughout. They were offering a secular education and it was constitutional for tax funds to support it.

Here is a fantastic business! A church comes into court pleading its right to tax funds on the ground that its schools have no religion in them, or an insignificant pittance of it at the most! If the facts support the pleadings, then the question immediately arises, why do the Catholics have separate schools at all? If their schools offer the same curriculum and teaching as the public system, why the duplication? Why not send their children to the public schools? And if the parochials are as hard up as described,

117

why do they not concentrate their declining resources on the teaching of religion? Why do they insist on carrying an impossible burden of secular education for the sake of one minuscule period of religion? They could actually get more religious opportunity in a program of released time from the public schools.

There is, of course, the possibility that the Catholic intervenors are misrepresenting the facts. It may be that they have more religion in their schools than they claim. After all, the directives of their top officials from the Popes on down, including Vatican Council II, are abundantly clear on this very point.[7] The schools are not to have just one course in religion; they are to permeate all courses, even physical education, with "Christian" — i.e. Roman Catholic — doctrine. Authoritative Catholic voices have again and again stressed what the *Southern Cross,* official diocesan publication of the San Diego diocese asserted in its Aug. 25, 1966, issue:

> Elementary and secondary state standards outline the curriculum to be followed in all California schools. The diocesan schools implement this curriculum in a religious atmosphere. In addition to religion being formally taught in the classroom, it permeates the teaching of every subject during the school day.

The Catholic lawyers may state in court that their schools are 90 per cent secular, but this is not what recruitment agents are telling the parents. An enrollment card to be filled out by parents seeking to register their children in the archdiocesan schools of Chicago contains the following:

> I wish to enroll my child in Saint Ferdinand School for September, 1969. I hereby pledge my cooperation with the teachers to whom I will trust my child for a program of Catholic education according to standards and directives established by the Archdiocese of Chicago.

In an address to the National Catholic Education Association, Rev. Thaddeus J. O'Brien, associate superintendent of schools of the Archdiocese of Chicago, had some clear statements to make about the Catholic nature of the Catholic school. As reported by *Religious News Service,* March 31, 1970, he said:

> The Catholic school must be Christian. It must be alive

118

with the Gospel message of love. . . . The rules of discipline, the style of life in the schools, the method of dealing with personal problems, all must be done in a Christian manner. . .

The Catholic school exists as a part of a large system which is the Church and must be grounded in the theology of the Church.

The Catholic school takes meaning and function from the Church herself. What the Church is, the school should be. . . . The school must serve the Church and in a special way, it draws its purpose, life and meaning from the Church which is Christ's body.

In his definitive work, "Catholic Education in the Western World," James Michael Lee of Notre Dame has this to say about the religious nature of Catholic schools:

In most Catholic schools, except possibly in major Catholic universities, attendances at certain religious exercises is a part of the religious instructional program of the school. Elementary schools normally require students to attend Mass one weekday and also to go to Confession. Time is provided within the regular school day for attendance at such exercises. Almost all parishes reserve one Mass on Sundays especially for the Catholic school children with a sermon prepared especially for them. . . . Some secondary schools . . . retain compulsory Mass or Confession during weekdays. . . . All Catholic schools at all levels gently urge frequent attendance at daily Mass and weekly Confession; all schools make concrete provisions for such opportunities.[8]

So, it may be that the Catholic schools are more religious than the court pleaders try to make out. It may be that the directors of these institutions are surreptitiously bootlegging religion into their program. Such speculation demonstrates about as well as anything what is wrong with state aid to church schools.

Can the argument of the Roman Catholic school as a predominantly secular institution, paralleling the public school and doing the same job, actually win in the High Court? The response of the Supreme Court to the constitutional question was a long time in coming, much longer than should have been the case. Plaintiffs anxious to test the federal aid laws, as well as state laws, in federal courts found themselves blocked by an unfortunate precedent es-

119

tablished a half century earlier. In the case of *Frothingham v. Mellon*, the right of citizens to bring suits as taxpayers was severely curtailed. The favored procedure to challenge constitutionality of federal expenditures had been to bring suit as a taxpayer, charging that tax funds were being spent in violation of law. But in *Frothingham* the Court held that a taxpayer's interest in such proceedings was not sufficient to give him "standing" to sue. The *Frothingham* opinion cast doubt upon the right of federal courts to entertain any suits challenging expenditures of federal tax money.

The frustration of church-state separationists was monumental. They saw the Congress passing and the President signing into law bills which seemed to them of highly dubious constitutionality. The same thing was going on in the states. Yet, in a dreary, succession of failures, taxpayer plaintiffs were turned down in federal court for lack of "standing to sue." Senator Sam J. Ervin, Jr. sought a way out of this impasse by an amendment to the Elementary and Secondary Education Act which would have given federal courts jurisdiction to entertain suits questioning the constitutionality under the First Amendment of federal grants to church institutions. Twice the Senate did pass such amendments by voice vote. But Rep. Emanuel Celler, chairman of the House Judiciary Committee, simply refused to do anything about the matter at all. The excuse he offered was that the Justice Department was opposed to the bill. Certainly the Catholic lobby was actively opposed to it and exerted strong pressure to keep it bottled up in Judiciary. This fact never came to public notice.

A thoroughly frustrated man, Sen. Ervin complained on the Senate floor:

> Why any man who has taken an oath to support the Constitution of the United States would consent to the Constitution of the United States being nullified insofar as the First Amendment is concerned. is something beyond my feeble intellect to comprehend.[10]

Eventually, the litigation impasse was broken. But by the time this happened the programs of government aid to church schools were off and running. They had had more than two years of operation, time to become ensconced in the bureaucracy and to gain some measure of toleration, if not acceptance, from the public. In *Flast v. Cohen* a 1968 case, the Court finally decided the standing issue in favor of the plaintiff.[11] The suit which challenged expenditures for church schools under ESEA had been thrown out on the standing issue in a split decision by a three-judge panel in district court. The issue was appealed to' the United States Supreme Court which proceeded to overturn the opinion of the lower court and grant standing to the plaintiffs to bring their suit. Chief Justice Warren wrote for the Court:

. . . the Establishment Clause of the First Amendment does specifically limit the taxing and spending power conferred by Article I, Par. 8 Whether the Constitution contains other specific limitations can be determined only in the context of future cases. However, whenever such specific limitations are found, we believe a taxpayer will have a clear stake as a taxpayer in assuring that they are not breached by Congress. Consequently, we hold that a taxpayer will have standing consistent with Article III to invoke federal judicial power when he alleges that congressional action under the taxing and spending clauses is in derogation of those constitutional provisions which operate to restrict the exercise of the taxing and spending power.[12]

Of course the *Flast* plaintiffs had to go back and start all over again, but the first big hurdle had been cleared. At least the church-state issue could be heard. Once the standing barrier to church-state First Amendment suits had been removed, such suits challenging virtually every program of government aid to church schools were filed in half a dozen states. The outcome of these lawsuits would determine the church-state picture in the United States for a long time to come.

The first of a series of strategic lawsuits to reach the Supreme Court was *Board of Education v. Allen,* a 1968 New York case.[13] The outcome did much to encourage churchmen whose dream of tax support for their institutions had, as a result of earlier opinions of the Court, appeared beyond the possibility of fulfillment. Undoubtedly the rash of federal legislation granting aid to church schools, followed by another rash of state legislation doing the same thing, had its effect. The legislation was accompanied by elaborate rationales of evasion and these, too, had their effect. Was this, indeed, the wave of the future? Did all of this signal a retreat by the Court from its tight money line construction of the First Amendment? This was the mood of *Allen;* at least this was the way *Allen* was initially interpreted by the lower courts which began to use it as justification for various kinds of direct subsidies to sectarian institutions.

Before getting into the *Allen* case, it is important to recall *Everson*. Let us reiterate that in finding transportation aid for Catholic students permissible the Court specifically denied all forms of school aid whatsoever. Busing could be financed by the state only because it was a safety aid to the child, and not an aid to the school's educational program. The statute conveyed a welfare aid. Only because it was over on the welfare side was it permissible aid.

The *Allen* case involved a constitutional challenge to a New York law passed in the wake of ESEA. The law was predicated on the idea that if the Federal Government could provide textbooks for church schools as it was doing under the Elementary and Secondary Education Act, a state government could do it also. The issue before the Court was whether a New York law providing that textbooks purchased with tax funds could be given to parochial school students without violating the First and Fourteenth Amendments to the Federal Constitution. The Court's finding greatly widened child benefit and carried it beyond welfare into the educational program itself.

The majority agreed with Justice White's opinion that church schools "pursue two goals, religious instruction and secular education." Justice White's opinion approved textbook aid on the ground that this aid was rendered only to the secular education offered in these institutions and not to the program of religious instruction. Carried to its ultimate limit, this doctrine would enable government to finance the entire curriculum of the church school, save for one small course bearing the label of religion.

In *Allen* the Supreme Court hinted at an entirely new money line interpretation of the First Amendment. The First Amendment was not violated if there were a legislative purpose with a primary effect which neither advanced nor inhibited religion and carried a secular benefit for children and parents. Justice White was construed as saying that any kind of general or nonreligious aid to a religious institution or, more properly, to the persons in it, could be constitutional, and constitutionality would be presumed, lacking any specific evidence of aid to religion itself. At least this was the way the lower courts began to interpret and apply the *Allen* doctrine. They completely ignored Justice White's emphasis on the particular fact situation in *Allen* and the church-state safeguards to which he pointed.

Let us look at Justice White's approach to the First Amendment problem in government subsidy to church schools as seen in the following:

> Nothing in this record supports the proposition that all textbooks, whether they deal with mathematics, physics, foreign languages, history, or literature, are used by the parochial schools to teach religion. No evidence has been offered about particular schools, particular courses, particular teachers, or particular books. We are unable to hold, based solely on judicial notice, that this statute results in unconstitutional involvement of the State with religious instruction or that #701, for this or the other reasons urged, is a law respecting the establishment of religion within the meaning of the First Amendment.[14]

The New York law was carefully drawn, as Title II of ESEA had been, with the idea of skirting the church-state issue. The picture one might get from reading the law is that of a great company of children coming to one central depository and borrowing books, much as they might do at any public library. How completely Justice White relied on this language can be seen in these words from his majority opinion:

> The law merely makes available to all children the benefits of a general program to lend school books free of charge. Books are furnished at the request of the pupil and ownership remains, at least technically, in the State. Thus, no funds or books are furnished to parochial schools and the financial benefit is to parents and children, not to schools.[15]

While this language was useful in coping with the constitutional problem of church-state, it had nothing to do with the operation of the Act. As the program got underway the church schools simply sent in their requests and the books were sent to them.

The Yale Law Journal, Vol. 79, No. 1, Nov., 1969 contains a comprehensive survey of the operation of the New York State textbook distribution. It finds that sectarian-slanted textbooks were being distributed at the expense of the state. Indeed, some of the books were overtly sectarian, heralding the virtues of a particular religious denomination. The study concludes at page 138:

> The Court never completely applied its "effect" test in *Allen.* Though the test adopted was a pragmatic one, necessitating a finding of fact, the opinion dealt only in abstractions. It was assumed that the administrators of the law would properly define permissible and impermissible state aid, and guard effectively against the latter. The Court was wrong.
>
> Sectarian textbooks are being purchased under the New York Textbook Loan Law. This is true not only because certain officials fail to abide by constitutional standards from time to time. Rather, it is true because the statute and its regulations fail to provide rational standards for review, assign the review responsibility to incompetent officials, and use procedures which often allow for the purchase of unreviewed textbooks.

As Justice Douglas noted in his dissent:

> The statutory system provides that the parochial school will ask for the books it wants. Can there be the slightest doubt that the head of the parochial school will select the . . . books that best promote its sectarian creed? . . . If the board resists, then the battleline between church and state will have been drawn. . . .[16]

But as Justice Douglas anticipated, there has been no resistance. The parochials get what they want. Thus the Court okayed a form of parochial school subsidy that penetrated to the very center of the educational process. It had gone a long way toward instituting a government subsidy doctrine of "separate but equal" for private, sectarian schools. In his dissenting opinion Justice Black, who had written the majority opinion in *Everson,* said this:

It is true, of course, that the New York law does not as yet formally adopt or establish a state religion. But it takes a great stride in that direction and coming events cast their shadows before them. The same powerful sectarian propagandists who have succeeded in securing passage of the present law to help religious schools carry on their sectarian religious purposes can and doubtless will continue their propaganda, looking toward complete domination and supremacy of their particular brand of religion. And it nearly always is by insidious approaches that the citadels of liberty are most successfully attacked.[17]

In his concurrence Justice Harlan indulged in a permissiveness that went well beyond Justice White. He wrote that "where the contested governmental activity is calculated to achieve nonreligious purposes otherwise within the competence of the State, and here the activity does not involve the State 'so significantly and directly in the realm of the sectarian as to give rise to divisive influences and inhibitions of freedom,' it is not forbidden by the . . . First Amendment."[18] In his dissent Justice Douglas addressed himself to the Harlan doctrine:

The state's "competence" in the areas of health, safety and welfare of the people would under that view permit it to fund a church's charity programs, pay for renovating dilapidated church buildings, and pay for the services and upkeep, such as janitors' salaries and utility bills, necessary to maintain church buildings in safe and healthful condition. Indeed, short of state-provided prayer books, sacramental wine, and the like, churches could, apparently, become virtual state dependencies.
Should that, unhappily, come to pass, then perhaps the church would in time become an administrative arm of the state.[19]

If church-state separationists were to take Justice Douglas' prognosis literally, their future would be bleak, indeed. This was not really a prognosis: it was a warning. Justice Douglas was pointing to what could be the ultimate end of the child benefit theory as the majority handled it in *Allen*. The Court itself has frequently acknowledged that the church-state line is an extremely difficult one to draw. Separationists can be grateful for more recent decisions which have served as a corrective to *Allen*. The majority doctrine in *Allen*, if pressed relentlessly, could mean the end of church-state separation.

The direction which the *Allen* doctrine could take is demonstrated by the opinion of a federal District Court in Connecticut in the case of *Tilton v. Richardson*.[20] This lawsuit sought to bar federal grants to four Roman Catholic colleges in Connecticut — Sacred Heart, Albertus Magnus, Fairfield University and Amhurst College. The suit asserted that these institutions were owned and directed by a church and that grants to them violated the establishment clause of the First Amendment. In this case a panel of three judges gave an opinion almost diametrically opposed to that rendered by the Maryland Court of Appeals in the earlier Maryland college case of *Horace Mann v. Maryland Board of Public Works* (see Chapter 5). In *Tilton* the lower court held that it made no difference whatsoever whether the institution given federal aid were a church institution or a secular institution. The only thing that mattered was the function to be aided. If the particular function to be aided were a secular function, then the nature, purpose and management of the institution would not matter.

The court noted that the announced purpose of the Higher Education Facilities Act (which was under challenge) had been "grants only for the construction of academic facilities to be used for secular purposes." The court went on to say:

> The purpose of the Act appears on its face. . . . It . . . is to increase the student enrollment capacity of the Nation's institutions of higher education through grants for construction of academic facilities; . . . and such declaration is based on congressional findings that there is an urgent need for construction of such facilities to enable these institutions to accommodate anticipated increases in student enrollments . . . . We do not believe it to be within our competence to question such findings. . . .
>
> The Act also meets the second requirement of a primary effect that neither advances nor inhibits religion. *The focus of this test as applied in Allen is the function, secular or*

religious, which the government aid subsidizes — not the
nature of the institutions, secular or religious, which receives
the aid.[21]

Here the circle is completed. We commenced with a doctrine
of the First Amendment which held in *Everson* that "No tax can be
levied to support any religious . . . institutions, whatever they may
be called, or whatever form they may adopt to teach or practice
religion." Now we have come to *Tilton* in which a federal court
holds that any church school can be subsidized by government,
provided only that the particular phase of the church program to
be aided is secular. This is done with a perfectly straight face as
though the latter were somehow a logical outgrowth of the former,
instead of its flat contradiction. Devious indeed is the working of
the judicial mind! The damage to church-state separation done by
the lower court in *Tilton* was offset, but only partially so, by the indecisive ruling of the Supreme Court to be analyzed later.

Note, now, the cases of *Brusca v. State of Missouri* and that of
Jackson v. State of California. The complaints in these cases
purport to follow in logical sequence the line the Supreme Court
took in *Allen.* The immediate objective in *Brusca* and *Jackson* was
to strike all state constitutional provisions barring tax support of
church institutions. The ultimate objective was full state support
for such institutions. The contention was that if aid is provided for
some students and schools, and if it could legally be provided for
all students and schools, then if all are not aided, the law discrimi-
nates against those not aided. They are denied equal rights.

Thus, the California petition charges that the state "failed and
refused to provide educational benefits to children of plaintiffs
attending nonpublic schools, although it had the means available
to provide such benefits via tuition voucher bills . . . and other bills
which have failed of adoption." The Missouri petition alleged that
the state "failed and refused to provide educational benefits to the
plaintiff-children attending nonpublic schools despite the fact that
it had the means available to provide such benefits via tuition grant
bills . . . and other bills which have failed of adoption." Thus, the
First Amendment which has historically protected the people from
a tax for religion is now cited as authority for its imposition! Once

127

the *Allen* logic is turned completely loose, this is the sort of thing that results. It could end in a doctrine that religion must be established in order to guarantee equal rights! Fortunately, this kind of logic was far more than the Supreme Court could take. It affirmed the dismissal of the lower court.

Sectarian hopes for such lawsuits were accepted by columnist Russell Kirk, May 19, 1970:

> If such state constitutional provisions should be overthrown, then parents of children in nonpublic schools would be free to work for state subsidies to their schools or for some other form of public assistance.
>
> If the Missouri (and California) plaintiffs are successful, their action would eliminate the necessity for constitutional amendments in several states before such aid could be enacted by state legislatures.

The kind of wishful thinking to which the *Allen* opinion gave rise is demonstrated by the discussion provided by Patrick S. Duffy in the Winter, 1970 issue of *The Catholic Lawyer:*

> The (Allen) decision paves the way for extended federal and state aid to parochial schools. Arguments favoring aid for secular textbooks are amenable to extended application in the educational world. In the field of educational technology a textbook has become a dated concept as a repository of knowledge, retaining little of its old form beyond that of a workbook that may or may not accompany televised or programmed instruction. . . . With government funds the parochial school could offer secular teachers competitive salaries while the parish would finance the teaching of religion.

In the wake of the *Flast* case, lawsuits in federal courts were quickly undertaken which challenged the principal government programs aiding sectarian schools.

An especially strategic case was that of *Lemon v. Kurtzman* in the United States District Court for Eastern Pennsylvania. The lawsuit supported by Americans United and other groups challenged as in violation of the First and Fourteenth Amendments a channeling of state funds into church schools via a program of purchase of secular educational services rendered by them. Such services included teacher salaries, textbooks, and instructional materials. In a split decision with Chief Judge Hastie dissenting, the three-judge panel upheld the program and dismissed the suit. In its opinion the court went well beyond child benefit as the Supreme Court had enunciated it in the *Allen* case, and sped boldly into the field of institutional subsidy:

> Nor do we find persuasive the argument that the child must be the direct beneficiary of government funds which support secular education. Such an approach would place form over substance in that a constitutional result would depend upon minute distinctions and technicalities. The child and society generally certainly benefit from the improvement of the secular education the child receives regardless of whether there is a direct payment or loan to him or to his parents or to his school or teachers. In our view the constitutional result should not and cannot wholly depend upon the identity of the payee. The use to which the funds are put must be the primary concern.[22]

It is evident that if the Supreme Court had accepted such thinking, little of the separation of church and state would remain. There would scarcely be any phase of organized church activity for which ingenious clerics could not exact support from the silent majority. Listen again as this doctrine is developed by the lower court in *Lemon:*

> We recognize that "private education . . . is playing a significant and valuable role in raising national levels of knowledge, competence and experience," and that the public's reliance on private education suggests that adequate *secular* education is being provided in these schools. We further recognize, as did the Supreme Court in *Allen,* that the State's interest in education may be sufficiently served by reliance on the *secular teachings which accompany religious training* in nonpublic schools.[23]

Under this doctrine tax funds could be used for the support of any religious school in its teaching of religion, providing only that the school accompanied this teaching with enough general or secular education to meet the standards of the state. The *Lemon* case was appealed to the Supreme Court which eventually over-turned the lower court in a unanimous opinion. Coming down with that in *Early v. DiCenso* June 28, 1971, this was of the utmost importance for church-state relations in the United States.

The *Lemon* case was made notable by a highly unusual devel-opment — the intervention of the Justice Department on the side of the church schools. If, as appears likely, the intervention via a brief *amicus curiae* was undertaken at the direct suggestion of the Presi-dent, this would clearly position the executive Branch against money-line separation of church and state. It would indicate the administration's desire to undermine the First Amendment ban on government aid to religious institutions and to remove the people's protection against a tax for religion. If this is a correct interpreta-tion, it can be described as the first time in history that the Justice Department intervened against the Constitution.

There was yet another curious aspect of the Justice Depart-ment's brief in *Lemon*. Normally, such a brief would be signed by the Solicitor General of the United States, Erwin N. Griswold. The *Lemon* brief was signed, instead, by the Acting Solicitor General. Why was this? Someone suggested that the Solicitor General was ashamed to sign such a brief!

Reaching the Supreme Court along with the *Lemon* case was *Earley v. DiCenso*. This was a Rhode Island case.[24] The plaintiffs challenged a Rhode Island law which provided for payment of 15 per cent of the salary of lay teachers in parochial schools. Plaintiffs charged that this statute "on its face and as applied violates the Establishment Clause of the First Amendment in that it constitutes compulsory taxation for the support of religion." They also set forth that this statute "prohibits the free exercise of religion in that it constitutes compulsory taxation for the support of religion." Plaintiff alleged, finally, that the law "primarily benefits the Roman Catholic parochial school system because 96 per cent of the nonpublic school children in the state are enrolled in that system" and "by and large, no nonreligious private schools are eligible to receive benefits under it."

In complete contradiction of *Lemon v. Kurtzman*, plaintiffs won a decisive victory in a three-judge federal District Court in

Providence. The judges agreed that such direct grants to a parochial school were indeed "substantial support for a religious enterprise." They also found that such grants "produced the kind of reciprocal embroilments of government and religion which the First Amendment was meant to avoid." Judge Raymond J. Pettine dissented on one point: he did not find that the Act constituted aid to religion. But he did agree it produced "excessive government entanglement with religion," and was, therefore, in violation.

The court's way of reasoning is evident in the following quotation from the opinion. To provide aid to secular teaching was actually to undergird the entire operation:

It seems clear to us that this essentially religious enterprise (the parochial school) cannot succeed without good teaching in secular subjects. If the quality of teaching falls too low, then not only will Catholic parents be reluctant to enroll their children, but the parochial schools would also run afoul of Rhode Island's education laws. Good secular teaching is as essential to the religious mission of the parochial schools as a roof for the school or desks for the classrooms.[25]

There were other separationist victories. In *Johnson v. Sanders,* supported by Americans United, American Civil Liberties Union, and other groups, a three-judge federal District Court in 1970 unanimously struck down a Connecticut law which had provided an initial $6 million for purchase of services in parochial schools. This decision was subsequently affirmed by the Supreme Court in 1971. Of the schools receiving the funds 210 of 263 were Roman Catholic.

In a sweeping opinion in *Seegers v. Parker,* though with a divided court, the Louisiana Supreme Court struck down as in violation of that state's constitution another of the purchase of services laws which had been passed for the benefit of parochial schools. The date of the decision was October 18, 1970. The law provided state compensation for materials and teacher salaries in these institutions. It was hastily rammed through the legislature by a lobby combination of segregationist groups and the state's Roman Catholic hierarchy. To any reasonable mind, the law appeared to contravene the Louisiana Constitution which states: "No appropriation of public funds shall be made to any private or sectarian school." The Court found that the law did make such an appropriation and was therefore unconstitutional. The court concluded (Supreme Court of Louisiana, No. 50870) that "the constitutionally improper degree of entanglement and pregnant involvement is effectuated under this legislation." The court added:

Although the demarcation line between church and state is often difficult to ascertain, the activity permitted by this legislation would be entanglement forbidden by the establishment clause of our Constitution and forbidden by the constitutional provision restricting legislative spending of public moneys.

Another solid win for the separationists came in the west in 1970. Anaconda, Montana is a city with strong parochi-ethnic traditions. A clerical group there put to referendum a proposal to use school funds to pay the salaries of lay teachers in a parochial school. The referendum carried by a very small majority. The result was immediately challenged in court by local citizens supported by Americans United. The lawsuit, *Chambers vs. School District No. 10*, 1970, resulted in an opinion of the Montana Supreme Court which forbade any use of public funds to pay salaries of teachers in a parochial school. The court quoted from Pope Pius XI in making clear the pervasive nature of religious teaching in Catholic schools and declared: "If this is the aim of the church, then it would not be possible to determine where secular purpose ended and the sectarian began."

The church-state picture was confused, to say the least. Obviously there was a great deal at stake as the Pennsylvania and Rhode Island cases reached the Supreme Court. The Court was, in effect, ruling on the entire concept of government aid to church schools in the form of purchase of secular services as it had been developed in half a dozen states. All these laws were based on the same premise — that a church school is basically a secular school providing educational service on the same basis as a public school, and that the small part of the training that is religious could be lopped off from the major functioning of the school and receive no tax support. This was the issue, and the Supreme Court met it head on and decided it in the *Lemon* and *DiCenso* opinions announced on June 28, 1971.

The Court's intention in these cases is quite evident. It was not singling out just one method of subsidizing religious schools that could not pass the constitutional test. It was not playing a game. It was seeking in an epoch-making manner to draw definable limits in this entire area of aid to church schools. It was trying to say to the advocates of parochial school subsidy: "This is it: definitely no farther." It was the Court's intention to curb what it called a "downhill thrust easily set in motion but difficult to retard or stop." In *Lemon* and *DiCenso* the Court sought in its own words to locate "exactly where the verge of the precipice lies." It made it abundantly clear that direct or indirect grants to support secular instruction offered in religious schools were well past the brink. What the Court sought in *Lemon-DiCenso* was to reverse the direction of *Allen.*

We should recall that the Pennsylvania and Rhode Island plans represented the ultimate in clerical circumvention. Some of the best legal brains of the nation had slaved at devising a strategy of evasion which would permit government subsidies for church schools. Every effort was bent toward walling off the so-called secular phase of the religious school and providing government subsidy for it only. Thus, there would be no aid to religion of the sort the Court had repeatedly found in violation of constitutional principles. The architects fondly supposed that they were presenting the Court with the perfect device for deserting its historic position and agreeing to a partial union of church and state.

No stone was unturned, no device neglected, nothing left undone that could have been done to secure this result. As the Court itself noted, at the trial level parochial school teachers went on the stand to testify that they never sought to inject religion into their teaching. Every kind of safeguard and precaution was provided to ensure that none of the government money would in any way support religious instruction or worship. But the Court did not say "Yes"; it said "No" with emphasis added.

The Court rested its opinion primarily on the "excessive entanglement" between church and state which it believed to be involved in the laws before it. This point alone was sufficient. The Court said: "We need not decide whether these legislative pre-

133

cautions restrict the principal or primary effect of the programs to the point where they do not offend the religion clauses, for we conclude that . . . the entire relationship arising under the statutes . . . involves excessive entanglement between government and religion." That is to say, the excessive entanglement was so clear and pronounced that the Court felt it need go no farther.

In its delineation of entanglement the Court had to indicate what it was that was entangled. In doing this the Court pointed to abundant evidence that parochial schools constitute an "integral part of the religious mission of the Catholic Church." Also that "they are a powerful vehicle for transmitting the Catholic faith in the next generation." But all such evidence was cited only as a means to an end. The end was to demonstrate excessive entanglement between state and church. The Court stated: ". . . the very restrictions and surveillance necessary to insure that teachers play a strictly non-ideological role give rise to entanglements between church and state."

Justice Burger's opinion for a unanimous Court makes it clear that any program of public subsidy to church schools which involves continuing ties, continuing inspections, continuing surveillance are unconstitutional since it is such entanglements that the First Amendment sought to prevent.

The Court called attention to its opinion in the *Walz* case where it upheld tax exemption for religiously used property.[26] It so held on the ground that there was no excessive entanglement in such exemption. The state grants tax exemption to the church and that is that. The whole thing is done and over with. The difference between this and the Pennsylvania and Rhode Island situations was that the latter set up a continuing series of relationships breeding entanglement. Such a condition must therefore be looked for carefully in any proposed state aid programs for parochial schools.

The Court held against parochial school subsidies on yet another ground: that of political division along religious lines. No doubt with the recent church-state political brawls in New York and Michigan and several other states in mind, the Court decried "the potential divisiveness of such conflict" and called it a "threat to the normal political process." This, it said, "was one of the principal evils against which the First Amendment was intended to

134

protect."

The Court sought to cut off this grim area of sectarian controversy in the firm understanding that far from receding, it would continue, like a cancer, to grow and expand. The Court stressed that in both Rhode Island and Pennsylvania church leaders had argued that the initial grants for their schools were not sufficient and that a great deal more would be required. The Court saw clearly "pressures for expanding aid" and decreed that such a progression should not be commenced. It realized that the financial interests of the church had already become a political issue, infecting the political process, diverting attention and effort from the spiritual mission of the church. Here was something bad, something that should not be approved and encouraged, but scotched once and for all.

The Supreme Court doctrine of the First Amendment as enunciated in the Pennsylvania and Rhode Island cases was speedily applied to other laws. The Supreme Court itself upheld the opinion of a federal District Court striking down a Connecticut purchase of services law for the benefit of parochial schools. This was announced June 30, 1971. In *Americans United v. Oakey* a similar Vermont law which allocated funds to parochial schools for instruction in science, mathematics and modern foreign languages was struck down. The opinion was handed down in federal District Court in January, 1972. A similar fate was met in federal court (a split decision 2 to 1) by a New York law under which state funds were paid to parochial schools for mandated services. Such services included counting the number of students in the school and other forms of record keeping. The decision was announced in April, 1972.[27]

Another New York law under which parochial schools were paid $33 million in support of their secular teaching program was struck down as unconstitutional. This was a January, 1972 decision by a federal District Court. It followed directly the logic of *Lemon*.

The decisions were basically similar and all took their rise from the Supreme Court's opinion in *Lemon* and *DiCenso*. The following passage from the opinion in the *Oakey* case demonstrates the court's conviction that such forms of public assistance as those under review did involve state aid to religion:

135

The sectarian mission of the church-based parochial school cannot be overemphasized. It is unlikely that such schools carried on under religious auspices could exist if it were not for that mission. Hence, the role of the dedicated teacher therein is paramount. . . . Even without overt attempts to influence the teaching program of the secular instructor, the teacher would still be subject to the subtle but effective pressure of parochial, administrative religiously oriented, parental approval.[28]

Hardly had this rash of decisions sounded the death knell of aid to secular education in church schools when new devices for aiding these institutions put in their appearance.

The new devices were tuition grants to reimburse parents of parochial school pupils and tax credits for tuition paid such an institution. There was also the voucher plan under which parents of a parochial school pupil would receive a certificate cashable against tuition in that school. The evasive stratagem common to all these proposals was that the government subsidy would pause a moment, at least theoretically, with the parent before it was deposited in the church school. It was argued that this aids the parent, not the religious institution. The parents' touch was supposed to sterilize the money and resolve the constitutional problem.

In the legislative sessions of 1970 and 1971, at least a dozen state legislatures were considering such proposals. We have also noted that a certain group within the Nixon administration favored federal aid to parochial and private schools either in the form of educational vouchers or tax credits for parents. These proposals have some appeal as a possible device to encourage the spread of private schools for the purpose of avoiding racial integration. They are appealing also for those who are dissillusioned with the public schools and ready to give up on them.

The only longtime American precedent for the tuition voucher program was one that had been in operation in Vermont from 1880 to the 1960s. South Burlington School District had no high school. It paid a tuition grant to parents who were thus required to send their children to high school in another district. The state also provided its per student share of such payments and the parent could select his own school — public or private. Some of the students were enrolled in Catholic high schools and drew the payments to these institutions. Americans United supported a taxpayer, C. Raymond Swart, in a court challenge to these payments.[29] It turned out to be a First and Fourteenth Amendment case since Vermont law was not very specific on the church-state question. The South Burlington School Board argued that no assistance to the religious schools was involved, that the board was only aiding parents who were required by law to send their children to school. Since there was no nearby school available, these parents were doing the best they could and the school district was doing the best it could to help them.

The Vermont Supreme Court found for the plaintiff in 1961, striking down the entire tuition grant program, holding that it exceeded the limits of the United States Constitution. The case was appealed to the United States Supreme Court which refused a hearing in the case, allowing the decision to stand.

The opinion of Justice James S. Holden concluded:

> Considerations of equity and fairness have exerted a strong appeal to temper the severity of the mandate. The price it demands frequently imposes heavy burdens on the faithful parent. He shares the expense of maintaining the public school system, yet in loyalty to his child and his belief seeks religious training for the child elsewhere. But the same fundamental law which protects the liberty of a parent to reject the public system in the interests of his child's spiritual welfare, enjoins the state from participating in the religious education he has selected.[30]

An advisory opinion handed down by the Massachusetts Supreme Judicial Court in June, 1970, fully agreed. In its 7 to 0 opinion the Massachusetts tribunal found that a proposed tuition grant program was in clear contradiction to the church-state provisions of the Massachusetts Constitution.

The indirect subsidy for sectarian schools provided by the parental tuition reimbursement program continued to encounter heavy going in the courts as new cases emerged. Pennsylvania became a prime battleground for the new parental reimbursement plan as it had been for the purchase of secular services. Here the

Catholic lobby had de facto control of the legislature and was able to pass any bill it wanted. A tuition reimbursement bill was promptly passed to replace the former purchase of services law.

In *Lemon v. Sloan* a three-judge panel unanimously ruled, April 6, 1972, against a motion to dismiss a challenge to the constitutionality of this law.[31] In its opinion on the motion the court virtually decided the case on its merits. The court held "in each case (of parental reimbursement) tax-raised funds are being used to subsidize religious education." The court ruled that "the state has no more power to subsidize parents in providing religious education for their child than it has to subsidize church-related schools to do so."

In a pivotal case, *Wolman v. Essex,* a federal District Court in Ohio struck down a law granting parents $90 per year for each child in a parochial or private schools for the years 1971-72 with future grants to be determined by the State Board of Education.[32] The federal court ruled, April 17, 1972, that ". . . payment to the parent for transmittal to the denominational school does not have a cleansing effect and somehow cause the funds to lose their identity as public funds . . ." This opinion was subsequently upheld by the Supreme Court.

Yet another plan for sectarian school subsidies is the tax credit. This plan would reduce a parent's state or federal income tax in recognition of payments for his child's tuition in a church school. A lower court in Minnesota upheld constitutionality of that state's tax credit law.[33] The case has been appealed to the Minnesota Supreme Court. In Ohio (January 1972) a federal court held that state's tax credit law to be in violation of the First Amendment (*Wolman v. Kosydar*). The Supreme Court will undubtedly deal with this issue in time.

The New York PEARL coalition of 25 organizations developed the plan of going into court immediately as each new parochiaid maneuver was undertaken by the legislature. The clerical strategy was to maintain a flow of state funds by passing one unconstitutional statute after another, the sponsors figuring on at least several months of benefits before the cut off could occur. When the New York Legislature and Governor Rockefeller put through a bill providing $4 million for repair and maintenance of church school buildings, the PEARL coalition was waiting for them. A

138

prompt suit brought a prompt and unanimous ruling in federal District Court that such payments were unconstitutional, (The ruling came down July 21, 1972) and the cut off was immediate. The three federal judges reserved decision on the constitutionality of another feature of the law which PEARL had also attacked. This provided tax credits for low income families with children in parochial schools. PEARL appealed to the United States Supreme Court.

In all such plans the money is ultimately channeled into the church school for its entire instructional program. This is true regardless of the particular conduit that is employed. Yet the Court has already held that even the financing of the secular instruction in the church school violates the First Amendment. How then could the new stratagem which aids the entire school hope to succeed? As for entanglement, that is certainly not lessened by the ensnarement of the parent in the financial and management triad of church, state and parent in combination to effect religious subsidies.

All of these devices, and others that ingenious minds may conceive, are means which seek to accomplish state aid to church schools by indirection. The Court has repeatedly held that what may not be done directly may not be done indirectly. While it is conceivable that a reversal of its entire previous position as set forth in *Everson, McCollum, Zorach, Torcaso, Engel, Schempp, Lemon* and *DiCenso* may come about, it seems more reasonable the Court will continue to insist that the line of separation between church and state be kept clear and firm. As of the moment, the admitted vagary of the *Allen* case has been corrected and the Court's position appears firm.

This bright picture for church-state separation may have been dimmed a bit by the Supreme Court's decision in *Tilton v. Richardson* which partially sustained the lower court and by the thinnest possible margin. The plurality opinion which upheld federal construction grants at four church-related colleges came down the same day as the finding in *Lemon* and *DiCenso*. It may change the *Lemon-DiCenso* picture a little, but not much.

The Court held that aid given to the four Roman Catholic colleges named in the suit did not involve aid to religion in the forbidden sense. At least this was not proved in the four instances brought before the Court. The Court repeatedly made it clear that it was deciding for the defendants because there was no specific evidence to indicate that the institutions were actually religious. Had the plaintiffs shown the sectarian permeation of these institutions which they alleged, the decision would have gone the other way, the Court implied. "There is no evidence that religion seeps into the use of any of these facilities," the Court said.

Then the Court outlined a view which is apparently destined to keep the issue in the courts for years on end:

> Individual projects can be properly evaluated if and when challenges arise with respect to particular recipients and some evidence is then presented to show that the institution does in fact possess these characteristics.[34]

Indeed, this language apparently did not rule out a further challenge to the very grants that had been litigated in *Tilton v. Richardson*. The plaintiffs immediately announced that they would go to court once more armed with specific evidence indicating the sectarian nature and control of the four colleges in question. Challenges to other church-related colleges that might openly avow their sectarian ties were indicated. A long and protracted period of litigation was promised for the grants to church-related colleges.

The majority, with Chief Justice Burger writing the opinion, did, however, clip off one part of the Higher Education Facilities Act as unconstitutional. In order to avoid the church-state issue, the law provided that no religious worship or instruction could be provided for a period of twenty years in buildings erected with federal funds. This was supposed to be the duration of the government equity in the buildings. The Court was dissatisfied, considered the protection against sectarian involvement inadequate, and directed that the ban on religious programs in those buildings be made permanent.

The state of public opinion on the issue of parochial school subsidies is an important aspect of the problem. If government suspects that the public is ready to abandon public schools in favor of state-subsidized sectarian and private schools, this feeling will be reflected in legislation. The feeling will also be reflected in the judiciary. All the polls that we have seen on government aid to parochial schools have registered a majority in opposition.

In 1969, for example, Gallup International did a nationwide survey using the question: "In some nations, the government allots a certain amount of money for each child for his education. The parents can then send the child to any public, parochial, or private school they choose. Would you like to see such an idea adopted in this country?" This survey showed 59 per cent responding "No," 37 per cent responding "Yes," and 4 per cent no opinion. Americans United Surveys conducted a survey in Maryland, March, 1970, using the same question. This showed 50.4 per cent opposed to government aid to religious schools, 46 per cent in favor, and 3.6 per cent no opinion. Realizing that the question was couched in terms designed to draw favorable responses, Americans United Surveys then conducted another sampling in Maryland using the following question: "Some state legislatures are considering legislation which would force all citizens, through taxation, to contribute involuntarily to the support of nonpublic schools. Most nonpublic schools exist mainly to teach the doctrines of particular religious denominations, and most of them in actual operation practice discrimination and selectivity along religious, racial, ability level, and socio-economic class lines. Do you approve or disapprove of legislation to provide tax aid to such schools?" This drew 81.9 per cent opposed and 17.5 per cent in favor, with 0.6 per cent no opinion.

Tests of voter sentiment on government aid to religious schools have been registered in New York (1967), Michigan (1970) and Nebraska (1970). Parochiaid was also defeated by the voters of Maryland, Oregon, and Idaho in three 1972 referenda. These highly significant results indicated massive popular sentiment against such schemes.

We have already analyzed in Chapter 4 the 1967 referendum in New York State which the separationists won by nearly 3 to 1. The importance of the church-state separation issue in the voting on the proposed charger cannot be over-stressed. It was the attempt to delete Article XI, Section 3, the peoples' protection against the tax for religion, that caught public attention. That was the crucial issue.

In Michigan there was a converse situation. Legislation providing basic forms of aid to church schools had already been passed by both houses of the legislature and had resulted in the fastening of this burden to the back of the taxpayers. Despairing of any relief from the Michigan court, a score of organizations banded together to petition for a referendum. These groups included many of the principal educational and religious organizations of Michigan. The largest Protestant groups of the state were well represented. Americans United was active in the consortium. The referendum provided a popular vote on the direct issue of public subsidies for sectarian institutions. It conceded the case for transportation to parochial schools at public expense. But with that single exception, it sought to bar public grants to churches or to any of their institutions or programs in the tightest conceivable language. The language deliberately set out to frustrate the various circumventions of the constitution with which we have become so familiar. The language which these groups brought to the voters in referendum was as follows:

No public money or property shall be appropriated or paid or any public credit utilized, by the legislature or any other political subdivision or agency of the state, directly or indirectly, to aid or maintain any private, denominational, or other nonpublic, pre-elementary, elementary, or secondary school. No credit payment, tax benefit, exemption or deductions, tuition voucher, subsidy, grant, or loan of public monies or property shall be provided, directly or indirectly, to support the attendance of any student or employment of any person at any such nonpublic school, or at any location or institution where instruction is offered in whole or in part to such nonpublic students. The legislature may provide for the transportation of students to and from any school.

The clerical leadership did everything possible to have the petitions invalidated by various technicalities and very nearly succeeded. Eventually, however, the petitions carried the parochiaid ban known as Proposal C to referendum on November 3, 1970. In its campaign to defeat Proposal C the Catholic hierarchy and the Christian Reformed leaders overreached themselves. Their misrepresentation was so crass as to create a backlash. It was proclaimed, for example, that the proposed amendment would deprive houses of worship of their tax exemption; that firemen would be barred from extinguishing a blaze at a church and police from protecting church property and personnel; that all federal school aid to Michigan would be cut off. Promoters of Proposal C were able to demonstrate the total falsity of such charges and the electorate simply refused to be deceived.

A roster of those recruited by the church school forces to oppose Proposal C is interesting. It included Henry Ford II, Edward Cole, President of General Motors, John Ricardo, President of Chrysler Corporation, Walker Cisler, chairman of the Board of Detroit Edison, both candidates for governor, both Michigan's United States senators, the state superintendent of public instruction, the atorney general and the mayor of Detroit. A Detroit *Free Press* poll published 10 days before the election showed Proposal C trailing by 56 per cent to 36 per cent with 8 per cent undecided. The result: Proposal C won by nearly 345,000 with 57 per cent of the vote.

In Nebraska, the outcome was even more decisive. Amendment 12 which would have authorized the legislature to fund up to one-third of the budgets of parochial schools, was defeated by 58 per cent of the vote, winning by a small margin in Omaha but losing badly in the rest of the state. The lesson of the referenda is clear: the people have a far surer instinct on church-state issues than do their political leaders. The people do not want to be taxed for church schools. When they are given the opportunity they will repudiate such proposals no matter how cleverly they are disguised. Both legislatures and courts should take cognizance of this.

Let us now relate directly to the issue raised at the begining of this chapter — namely the role of the courts in our political system. How is the judicial check and balance working? Legislators, it is said, can be pressured into passing unconstitutional bills. The President or the governor can similarly be pressured into signing them into law. But the Supreme Court, removed from the moil of politics, sitting in an atmosphere of judicial calm, can see the issue clearly and provide a sure defense for constitutional principles.

We have seen enough to realize that this is not quite the role the Supreme Court has played in our political history. There is a certain degree of subjectivity in its opinions. From time to time the

Court has evidenced a penchant for reflecting in an opinion what it took to be a popular consensus on a subject. Are we now to witness other examples of opinion which reflect a fancied consensus? Is Justice White's opinion in *Allen* an instance in point? Here the Court seized upon child benefit and spun it out well beyond reasonable limits. Does *Allen* reflect the feeling that the "Catholics have been having a hard time" with their schools and a way ought to be found to give them a little help? Are *Lemon* and *DiCenso* evidence that the pendulum has now swung the other way? Certainly the aggressive legislative and political campaign mounted by the Roman Catholic hierarchy to obtain funds is known. And the justices are well aware of the disposition of legislators to succumb to these pressures. Are they equally aware of grassroots sentiment, including a good deal of Catholic opinion, on the issue of government aid to church schools? These are pressures which are not without significance in shaping the decisions of the Court. It seems evident that such pressures on the clerical side must be promptly matched by counter-pressures if separation of church and state is to survive the current challenge. The Michigan and Nebraska referenda offer signs of a turning tide in church-state issues. It may be that the people have had enough. This is encouraging, for public opinion itself is the court of last resort.

The litigation since *Lemon-DiCenso* provides further evidence of a turning tide, or more properly, a re-turning tide. We have examined the decisions in a number of these cases. These opinions demonstrate that it is still possible for the Supreme Court to stiffen the no-establishment doctrine in time to save the public schools and protect the country from a *de facto* establishment of religion.

There are, however, significant issues that have yet to make their way to the Supreme Court. Plaintiffs in these cases must carry a heavy burden. They must be prepared to establish more clearly than they did in *Allen* and *Tilton* the religious motivation and direction of the denominational school. They must articulate the violation in the government's use of the church to accomplish secular purposes when alternative methods are available. They must show the indispensable importance of good secular education to a religious school. They must pitilessly trace the conduit principle by which both tuition grants and tax credits channel public funds into sectarian schools.

144

Again, plaintiffs must demonstrate that if the state aids the church school, constant surveillance by the state is necessary, thus leading to entanglement. But if there is no surveillance, aid to religion is inevitable. Plaintiffs must not shrink from demonstrating the basic importance of the church school to the church itself. Such pleadings are not easy, but this is the kind of burden the church-state plaintiffs must bear if they expect to preserve the separation of church and state.

The path of the defendant denominational schools as they defend their state subsidy in court is also clear. In order to defend themselves against the charge of religious permeation they must rapidly de-religionize their schools. They must purge all instruction and exercises, and all teaching instruments, equipment and symbols that would tend to promote religion. They must confine religious instruction rigorously to a small sector of their curriculum. They must be prepared to stand official inspection of their institutions at this point. No doubt charges will be regularly leveled that the church schools are including religion with their secular courses financed by the taxpayers, and the church must be ready to demonstrate that this is not the case. Certainly a dilution of clerical control of governing boards would be indicated. Schools owned and administered by clerics can hardly be made to appear as public institutions offering secular instruction. Public accountability on finances will also be required. How can a church seek public aid for its institutions while refusing to make public its resources?

Notes

1. *Everson v. Board of Education*, 330 U.S. 1 (1947)

2. *McCollum v. Board of Education*, 330 U.S. 203 (1948)

3. *Ibid*.

4. *Zorach v. Clauson*, 330 U.S. (1952)

5. *Engel v. Vitale*, 370 U.S. 421 (1961)

6. *Americans United v. Essex*, Court of Common Pleas, Franklin Co., Ohio, No. 232,751

7. E.G., Pius XI, *Christian Education of Youth*, 1929

8. Lee, James Michael, *Catholic Education in the Western World*, University of Notre Dame Press, 1967, p.291

9. *Frothingham v. Mellon,* 262 U.S. 447 (1923)

10. *Congressional Record,* December 16, 1968

11. *Flast v. Cohen,* 392 U.S. 83 (1968)

12. *Ibid.*

13. *Board of Education v. Allen,* No. 660, October Term, June 10, 1968. In the Supreme Court, 392 U.S. 236 (1968)

14. *Ibid.*

15. *Ibid.*

16. *Ibid.*

17. *Ibid.*

18. *Ibid.*

19. *Ibid.*

20. *Tilton v. Richardson,* Civil Action No. 12,767, March 19, 1970, U.S. Dist. Court, District of Connecticut. Affirmed by Supreme Court June 28, 1971 — 312 F Supp. 1191

21. *Ibid.* emphasis added

22. *Lemon v. Kurtzman,* Civil Action No. 69-1206 U.S. District Court, Eastern District of Pennsylvania. Reversed by Supreme Court, Law Week 48.49.P.310 (F Supp. 35)

23. *Ibid.* emphasis added

24. *Earley v. DiCenso,* 316 F Supp. 112 (1971)

25. *Ibid.*

26. *Walz v. Tax Commission of New York City,* 397 U.S. 664 (1970)

27. *P.E.A.R.L. v. Rockefeller,* Civil Action No. 70 Civ. 2531, April 27, 1972.

29. *Americans United v. Oakey,* U.S. District Court for Vermont Civil Action No. 6393, 40 U.S.L.W. 2597 QUT.

29. *Swart v. South Burlington School District,* 122 Vt. 177, Cert. Denied, 366 U.S. 925 (1961) 425

30. *Ibid.*

31. *Lemon v. Sloan,* Civil Action No. 71-223, April 6, 1972

32. *Wolman v. Essex,* Civil Action No. 71-396, April 17, 1972

33. *Minnesota Civil Liberties v. State of Minnesota,* File No. 379526, File No. 380252

34. Op. cit.

7. The Churches Strike It Rich

A recent survey indicated that government at all levels is financing the churches to the tune of about $7 million annually. [1] As is invariably the case with federal programs, one thing always leads to another. What was done yesterday sets a precedent for doing something today and something else tomorrow. We see government money currently flowing to churches in the following federal aid programs: Hill-Burton (hospital) programs, health services, Elementary and Secondary Education Act, Adult Vocation Education, other education programs (over 150 in all). Economic Opportunity Act, Housing and Urban Development, surplus commodities and property donations, research development, and foreign aid. In addition, there is a multiplicity of state and municipal aid programs to churches in such categories as transportation, textbooks and various educational services for church schools, teachers' salaries and school equipment welfare aid, and also urban renewal programs in which municipalities share responsibility with the federal government.

None of these programs is undertaken as aid to a church institution. None of them mentions churches as eligible recipients of the funds. Many of them contain specific renunciations of aid for any program of worship or sectarian instruction. The programs are avowedly designed for purposes quite different from that of government subsidy to religion. The public is informed that the programs are designed to help children, cure poverty, buttress the

147

nation's health, care for the elderly, provide decent housing, clear slums, assist national defense, and offer other commendable forms of service. Yet in every one of these programs the churches have become deeply involved with government as the recipients of its patronage. Each program was presented and sold to the public with its own plausible rationale. Put them all together and the total effect is to sustain with tax funds a vast institutional spread of the church — a kind of backdoor establishment of religion.

The oldest of the church subsidy programs initiated by the Federal Government was the Hill-Burton Act which provided aid to sectarian hospitals. The program was passed and signed into law in 1946, went into effect in 1947, and has been steadily increased and widened during the years since. At first, Hill-Burton merely provided aid for hospital construction. In 1949, it was expanded to include research, experiment and demonstration programs. In 1954, it was expanded again to provide for construction of nursing homes. In 1958, to accommodate the Baptists who were nervous about government subsidies, long-term, low-interest loans were offered as an alternative to grants. Subsequent legislation has steadily increased the funds for all categories of hospital and medical aid.

The Hill-Burton concept offers the clearest possible example of what James Madison called the use of the church by the state "as an engine of civil polity." The state wanted to increase the nation's hospital facilities. The church was already in the hospital business. Therefore, the state would hire the church to expand its facilities, and, indeed, to provide new facilities for hospital care. Funds were, of course, made available for public hospitals as well. But over half the funds have gone consistently to the private, nonprofits and of these the largest category by far has been the religious. Cumulative totals running from 1947-1958 show the following breakdown of sectarian grants:

Church Affiliated Projects:

Roman Catholic	413
Protestant	167
Jewish	26
Total	606

148

Federal Contributions:

Roman Catholic	$168,643,000
Protestant	58,854,000
Jewish	9,467,000

Total $236,964,000

Across the nation spacious and modern temples of healing have been erected by the Federal Government to be owned and operated by churches.

The preponderance of Roman Catholic grants may be explained by the reluctance of some Protestant bodies — notably the Southern Baptists — to receive government aid. There have been instances where other churches have refused Hill-Burton funds. A remarkable case of this involving the Presbyterian Church occurred in 1962. A federal grant of $350,000 had been arranged by the staff of Presbyterian Convalescent Hospital at Broomall, Pa., and was referred to the Presbytery of Philadelphia for routine approval. Instead, the Presbytery turned it down. In a spirited debate, opponents cited the dangers of federal control of their institution and stated the opinion that Presbyterians should carry full responsibility for their own hospital.

But such episodes were rare exceptions. Grants to churches for their hospitals became routine through the 1950s and 1960s. When President Nixon tried to check the Hill-Burton largesse by vetoing its extension in 1970, both Houses of Congress passed the bill over his veto with thunderous majorities. The government has insisted on open admissions for the institutions aided and there have been lawsuits over this. But a far more serious problem concerns government subsidy to hospitals which are bound by a restrictive, sectarian code in their medical practice.

Of particular concern are the numerous grants to Roman Catholic hospitals which have such medical eccentricities as a rule flatly banning therapeutic abortion even when necessary to save the life of the mother. As many as 2,000 American women may have died unnecessarily each year because of this rule. The sectarian medical code applicable in Roman Catholic hospitals also prohibits any dissemination of birth control information and equipment even in cases where another pregnancy may jeopardize a woman's life. Physicians using the hospital facilities are bound by this restriction. The Catholic code forbids "all operations, treatments and devices to render conception impossible" and holds that "advising or otherwise encouraging contraceptive practices is not permitted."[2]

There have been numerous episodes in Catholic hospitals featuring the rigid enforcement of such sectarian restrictions upon physicians and patients. All of this creates doubts as to the constitutionality and the wisdom of providing government subsidies to hospitals operating under such a restrictive medical code which forbids therapies that are routine in other hospitals and approved by the code of the American Medical Association.

The fact that this is no medieval problem but a painfully contemporary one is quickly demonstrated. When New York finally eased its obscurantist ban on abortions and opened the way for operations of this kind in the hospitals of the state, the Roman Catholic Bishop Walter P. Kellenberg of the Rockville Centre Diocese promptly reminded Catholic physicians, nurses and other medical personnel that they would be excommunicated from their church if they had any part whatever in the performance of abortions. The *New York Times* of June 19, 1970, quoted Bishop Kellenberg as saying in explanation of his ban: "Direct killing of the innocent, whether born or unborn, is against the law of God."

The reaction of the Brooklyn Diocese was terse and to the point. A Catholic doctor who performs an abortion under the new law "can expect to be excommunicated," a diocesan spokesman declared.

When the American Medical Association proposed an easement of its own policies in regard to abortions, Roman Catholic authorities were quick to insist that such medical practice would never be permitted in Catholic hospitals and that if it were insisted upon, these hospitals would close. The *Washington Evening Star,* June 20, 1970, quoted the Rev. James T. McHugh, director of the Family Life Division of the United States Catholic Conference, as saying that easing the ban on abortions was a "drastic encroachment on the freedom of hospitals and the people who operate them." With nearly one-third of the hospital beds of the nation in Catholic institutions, the dimensions of this problem are apparent. Father McHugh declared: "The church will practically be forced to close its hospitals."

Archbishop John Peter Davis of Santa Fe, New Mexico, immediately reacted to a liberal abortion law passed by the legislature of that state. He stated (*Religious News Service* June 24, 1970) that any Catholic hospital would have to consult him before any abortion whatever could be performed. "Our stand on abortions has not changed," he said. "We are absolutely opposed to abortions and that is it in a nutshell." This is the kind of result that can be expected when medieval theological concepts are given precedence over modern medical practices.

This problem arises in the case of Marquette University Medical School in Milwaukee. The school sought state subsidies but these were barred by a tight provision in the Wisconsin Constitution. Whereupon the medical school undertook to divorce itself from the clerical control which had inhered in its relation with Marquette University, a school owned and managed by the Roman Catholic Society of Jesus. The school changed its name from Marquette University Medical School to Marquette Medical School, diluted the clerical contingent among the trustees and generally played down Catholic influence.

After taking such steps, the attorney general ruled that the institution had changed its status to nonsectarian to the degree necessary to pass muster with the constitutional provisions and receive $3.2 million in state aid. But there was one missing link in all this: would the Catholic code still apply to the medical practices at the school? An inquiry to Attorney General Robert W. Warren elicited the acknowledgement that no stipulation regarding this matter had been given. He stated that "the stipulation does not include a specific reference to the sectarian medical code . . ." It thus appears possible that the code may still be in force at this medical school and the hospital facilities it commands. It may be that Wisconsin taxpayers are paying for an incomplete medical service at an institution that in part is bound by an antiquated code. This is an issue that the courts may one day be called on to adjudicate. (Since the above was written this issue has appeared in court actions involving Catholic hospitals in Billings and Miles City, Montana.)

Let us have a look at the program of donations of government surplus property and urban renewal. The churches have profited handsomely from both. These two federal programs are entirely separate and distinct. Yet they have both resulted in the donation to the churches, free or at a nominal price, of valuable property which they will be able to use tax-exempt in perpetuity. The land may be given in a program of slum clearance or because it is presumed the church can put it to a worthy use. But the effect is the same: highly valuable real estate comes off the tax rolls as the domain of the church expands.

Consider the matter of surplus donations. After World War II the Federal Government found itself with a wide variety of bases, installations and equipment for which it had no use. Interested parties came up with the idea of having the government donate all of this surplus to nonprofit operators whose educational and welfare activities presumably served a public purpose. When the donations were passed out churches were at the head of the line. They reaped a rich harvest — multiplied millions in lands and buildings which the government turned over to them free, or for a small part of their true value. Since all of this was tax-exempt, the community could expect no return for its services. The church or church school or other church institution did, of course, render a service, but it was always a service with the sectarian flavor and purpose of the operator. From the church-state point of view, here was another federal program of massive aid to the churches.

Take the case of Loyola University, a Roman Catholic institution of the Jesuit Fathers near Chicago. Loyola wanted to expand. Especially it wanted a large site for its medical school. The schools's administrators coveted a handy site belonging to the Veterans Administration at Hines, Illinois. There were 60 acres in the tract which was valued at $4.8 million. Loyola was well able to buy the site at a fair value and, indeed, had funds reserved for land acquisition, but found a way to get the site for nothing. Its first plan was to slip a bill through Congress giving it the land outright. Such bills were actually introduced by the late Sen. Everett Dirksen, Sen. Paul Douglas and Rep. E.R. Finnegan. Hostile public reaction forced withdrawal of the bills and the quieter, administrative route was chosen.

Father James F. Maguire, president of Loyola, went to Veterans Administrator John S. Gleason, Jr., a member of his Loyola

Advisory Board. Gleason promised to get the Hines site for Loyola without charge. He undertook to get a government declaration that the Hines site was excess to VA needs. Fred B. Rhodes, Jr., VA general counsel and a Baptist who believed in church-state separation, balked at the deal and refused to provide the necessary certification. Besides, he knew that the Hines property was not really excess or surplus and would shortly be needed in its plans. At that point Rhodes was ousted from his job and a Catholic, Cyril B. Brickfield, replaced him. Mr. Brickfield promptly approved the proposal. All hands hotly protested that the Hines-Loyola deal had nothing to do with the job changes. But these are the facts and the facts speak for themselves.

Next man to handle the Hines-Loyola deal was Bernard L. Boutin, head of General Services Administration, who quickly gave his okay. He declared that the Hines land was surplus to government needs. Secretary Abraham Ribicoff of HEW gave his commitment to Father Maguire and Mr. Gleason. HEW officials then went through their meaningless routine of reviewing bids for the land and the award to Loyola was soon announced.

Public indignation over the giveaway to Loyola mounted high. As a sop to public opinion, 30 acres of the tract were turned over to the State of Illinois for a mental hospital. But the end of this bizarre deal was not yet. The donation was carried out in 1962. Within less than a year, the Veterans Administration which had blithely given assurance that the Hines property was excess to its needs was announcing that it had immediate need of substantial acreage for a new hospital in the Chicago area. The Veterans Administration did, in fact, pay $18.5 million of the taxpayers' money for a new site inferior to the one it had given away. The author can well remember the squirming letter from the Veterans Administration, still under Mr. Gleason's leadership, trying to explain why it would proclaim valuable acreage excess and give it away to a church, only to use taxpayers' money a few months later to buy more land in the same area. The Veterans Administration never explained, for there was no explanation. Such are the wonders of church-state relations when an aggressive church goes to work on a compliant government.

Certainly there can be no question as to the church involvement. At the time of the Hines acquisition the governing board of

Loyola was composed 100 per cent of Jesuit priests. Everyone of them was under vows of poverty and total obedience to the superior general. It is true that Loyola was committed to use the land for a medical school. But the medical school was not only owned lock, stock and barrel by the priests, its teaching program and practice actually had a sectarian coloration. We have already noted the Roman Catholic teaching that a therapeutic abortion can never be performed in a Catholic hospital even when necessary to save the life of the mother. Also its teaching that the use of contraceptives is sinful and wrong even in a case where conception might jeopardize a woman's life. Such teaching and practice, though it may be ignored in some situations, has a definite and obvious bearing on the question of using public property and funds for a Catholic hospital.

Government aid to the Loyola project by no means ended with the donation of the Hines property. The university boomed from that moment. First, the school was able to sell at a handsome profit the site it had originally acquired for its medical school but no longer needed. This was sold at an appreciated price of $2 million. Then the school obtained two separate federal grants of $732,000 and $685,000, plus a long-term loan of $2.7 million. And there have been various other forms of government aid.

A sister Catholic institution, the Jesuit St. Louis University, obtained in 1960 a vastly enhanced site via the condemnation power and financial aid of government. This was an urban renewal deal. Under a program of this kind there is supposed to be a community consensus that a certain area of the city is blighted and needs to be redeveloped. Then the selected area is bought up with the use of two-thirds federal money and one-third municipal money. This is done by mutual agreement if possible; by condemnation proceedings, if necessary. The area is then cleared of buildings and resold to selected developers who will provide the desired service and product for the community. Among prospective purchasers are, of course, the churches which are given a preferential non-profit user rate. While few would advocate exclusion of churches from redevelopment areas, there are serious questions raised by the manner of their participation.

There is the question as to whether churches involved in such

154

programs are given preferential treatment of the kind that might characterize establishment of religion. Then, there is the practical question of which churches will be included in the project and which will be excluded. In Pittsburgh's Allegheny Center project area there were fourteen churches. The government administrators decided to eliminate eleven and keep three. One church marked for elimination was actually told that if it was determined to stay as a user in the redevelopment, it would have to open its communion table to the general public! In the Diamond Heights project in San Francisco, of many churches all were eliminated save three. Is this the kind of decision government officials ought to be making?

In the case of the Mill Creek redevelopment project in St. Louis the doubts multiply. For this project scarcely nodded to the amenities of the redevelopment program. It was tailor made from the start for the Roman Catholic St. Louis University, though it also included acreage for the Christian Board of Publications which was thus able to expand greatly its property and operations. A complete plan of the 22.4 acre site as it was to be acquired and developed by St. Louis University was being circulated by the school long before the land had been purchased or the buildings razed. Any bidding by other potential users was nothing but a farce since it was understood that the school was to get the land. The specifics for use were drawn to fit its proposals and no one else would have had any chance. By means of the urban renewal program, St. Louis University, a wholly owned and controlled church school, was able to acquire a large tract of valuable land and to enhance greatly its operation in that city. St. Louis University paid only $535,000 — a small fraction of the property's real value. Other church users also received a discount rate for development land.

The Missouri Supreme Court upheld the giveaway sale by the Renewal Authority to St. Louis University on the ground that what the university bought was something of much less value than that acquired by the Authority. This meant that the court was willing to overlook the use of eminent domain on the part of the city to acquire the land and the cost of clearing the land of presumed slums. This acquisition and preparation of the land for use by the school's operators, with all its church-state overtones, was simply ignored. Though the state had admittedly exerted its basic power to enhance a church institution, the court could see here no constitutional violation. The case was not appealed to the United States Supreme Court. The land bargain was only the beginning of government largesse. A spot check made midway in 1962 indicated that St. Louis University had already received nearly $2 million in federal grants in various categories. A substantial part of the school's budget and expansion program has been financed by the Federal Government ever since. As this was being written, St. Louis University was pressing for one grant alone that totaled $9 million. There would seem to be no doubt the school would get it. Federal aid in a dozen additional categories was flowing into this institution which constantly complained of its poverty.

Even the very title of the program was misleading and inaccurate. It was supposed to be a program of urban renewal or urban redevelopment necessary for slum clearance. But what happened in virtually all the programs was that the tenants of the area were evicted with little or no provision for their resettlement. Since they could not afford the high rents in the renewal area they simply went elsewhere and created other slums.

Perhaps the classic use of urban renewal to enhance a church institution is to be seen in Pittsburgh where the Holy Ghost Fathers, a Roman Catholic order which operates Duquesne University, was the recipient of government largesse at the hands of the Pittsburgh Urban Redevelopment Authority. A small Catholic school atop the bluff in Pittsburgh, Duquesne decided to go big-time. But there was a problem. All the land in the area was already occupied by homes and small businesses. The urban renewal program must have been viewed by this school as a literal godsend. On the face of it, such a program was a misnomer, even absurd. The bluff when the author first viewed it just before the renewal holocaust was in no sense a depressed area. It was a sturdy, middle-class community and there was nothing blighted about it. But Duquesne wanted to expand and that meant that the homes and businesses had to be taken and their tenants evicted. Here, again, was the use of government's eminent domain on behalf of a church institution.

One of the curious things about the bluff renewal project was the way its authors shifted gears and figures in a manner to leave

156

any observer quite confused. For example, the *Pittsburgh Press,* May 31, 1959, stated that the project would involve 58 acres and that 445 families and 135 businesses would be evicted at a cost of $7 million. But the same paper reported on March 7, 1962, that the project would involve 22 acres and that 44 families and 54 businesses would have to be evicted. Now, however, it was reported that the cost would be $10,745,915. That is, the project had been reduced by more than one-half while the cost had been increased by one-third! There was no explanation. What apparently happened, however, was that everything in the project except the Duquesne enhancement had been abandoned.

There were no competitive bids by other prospective educational users. This was an operation conceived and tooled for Duquesne. The announced price that Duquesne was supposed to pay was $954,000. The cost of razing the buildings on the land — $185,005 — was borne by the Urban Development Authority. As soon as it had acquired the land, Duquesne announced a $20 million development program. Most of this money was expected from the federal government in the form of construction grants. When the writer visited the campus in the early stages of this development, he observed signs at various projects announcing that they were being built with federal aid.

Is Duquesne a church institution? At the time of the urban renewal program in 1962, Duquesne had a governing board composed entirely of Catholic priests, members of the Holy Ghost Fathers. The president of the school was a priest of the same Order. The ex-officio chancellor of the university was the diocesan bishop. The buildings were replete with sectarian symbols and indicia and uniformed religious were everywhere. Here in the heartland of one of the nation's great cities, federal and municipal governments cooperated in an urban renewal program which established a religious institution in a place of prestige and influence.

It might be of interest to note in passing the methods used by the Holy Ghost Fathers and the Renewal Authority to evict the tenants of the area and secure their property. The moment the program was announced deterioration of the area began. The bluff area of Pittsburgh had been a solid, middle-class community. But when the author visited it in 1964 it had already become a ghost town full of rat infested dumps and drooping structures. The government's power of eminent domain had to be invoked in only a few instances. Once panic had begun to spread through the community, the tenants folded up, one by one, taking what they could get and leaving. Here and there one encountered a stubborn hold-out. But when his neighbors were gone and he was surrounded by decaying, boarded up buildings marked for the bulldozer, his determination would fade. Before long, he too, was ready to sell and get out.

The bitterness of the evicted residents of the area against the Holy Ghost Fathers was very great. The press carried a number of stories during 1962 describing the fury with which some of these citizens defended their homes and businesses. The *Pittsburgh Press*, July 3, 1962, for example, copiously reported a public hearing at which the wrath of the residents was particularly directed against the religious order which was evicting them. Attorney H.A. Sherman, representing Leonard and Josephine Scarpino, denounced the procedures under which his clients were being ousted from the area as unconstitutional. He asserted that it is a "perversion of power of condemnation by an authority, which openly, patently proposes to take property and turn it over to another party for private use." It takes private property "for a sectarian institution and uses public funds for the benefit of an institution furthering the principles of a religious faith."

Mrs. Thomas K. Delahanty denounced the injustice of Duquesne University in the destruction of her home. "This was a conspiracy for 12 years," she charged, accusing the school of planning that long for the acquisition of the area. Another critic, Abe Brenner, pointed out that the land which Duquesne was to acquire "will never again bring in taxes . . ."

There is yet another church-state problem involved in deals like that between the City of Pittsburgh and the Holy Ghost Fathers. Like most large American cities, Pittsburgh had been plagued in recent years with a rapid increase in tax-exempt property. In 1968-1969 Pittsburgh assessment records disclosed that 32.7 per cent of the city's property was exempt from tax, and that this percentage was increasing. It is likely that the figure now approaches 50 per cent. Of all the exempts, 20.6 per cent were religious, and that figure, too, has since grown. Urban renewal programs with a heavy accent on exempt users were at least partially responsible for this situation. The rise of tax exemption in proportion to taxable property meant that in a day of ever increasing demand for services, the revenue base for providing them was on the decline. The bluff project alone took 22 acres of highly valuable land off the tax rolls and substantially reduced the city's revenue.

There were two or three other massive religious expansion programs via urban renewal that are worthy of mention. Two of them involved the Society of Jesus, a Roman Catholic order. In one of the earlier renewal programs Fordham University received land for a new campus on a highly valuable site at Lincoln Square in New York City. Also included in the project were St. Matthews Church and Grace Institute, both Roman Catholic. The proposed project involved 18 square city blocks, a $228 million redevelopment. The proposed costs were $42 million for the Federal Government and $21 million for the city. Fordham was to acquire 300,000 square feet. Its bid for the property was $5 a foot which a lawsuit subsequently charged would involve a subsidy of at least $3½ million to Fordham. Because of the bitter public controversy and the lawsuit, the price to Fordham was subsequently raised to about $7 a foot. The cost of acquisition was about $20 a foot.

The project was touch and go for a considerable period as long-time residents of the area fought eviction. Serious doubts about the project were expressed by Albert M. Cole, Federal Housing Administrator. He called for a new appraisal of the land values by independent appraisers. Cole was publicly denounced by Robert Moses, chairman of the New York City Committee on Slum Clearance, who was determined to drive the Lincoln Square project through. Moses called Cole a bigot. He urged the Fordham people to go to Washington and take their case directly to President Eisenhower. They did so. Cole quickly changed his mind, said no independent appraisal would be necessary. Moses was jubilant. In the *New York Times*, August 9, 1957, we read that "Mr. Moses hinted that the withdrawal of the demand for new appraisers was connected with the visits or calls to Washington by some influential backers of the project." The lawsuit challenging the Fordham deal on church-state grounds resulted in a ruling which favored Fordham. In the New York Court of Appeals the opinion was written by Chief Justice Desmond, a man who for years publicly advocated state subsidies to church institutions. He based his decision on the premise that the markdown to Fordham was justified since ". . . what the city bought is not the same as what Fordham bought." This writer pointed out at the time (Feb. 19, 1963) in a letter to William L. Slayton, Urban Renewal Commissioner:

> The contention that "What the city bought is not the same as what Fordham bought" is true, but only in the sense that what Fordham bought was something much better. Fordham had a site cleared of slums (sic) and capable of vast development for the church which owns and operates that institution for its own purposes.
> Do we understand you to argue that the land was far more valuable with the "slums" than when ready to serve the purposes of the church which acquired it? If so, what is the use of a program which depreciates urban land values?

Another prime example of church institutional enhancement was provided by the Marquette University urban redevelopment program in Milwaukee. As a result of this program, Marquette, a Catholic institution of the Society of Jesus, was able to increase its campus from 28.8 acres to 61.2 acres. Cost to the Federal Government was $15,711,910; net cost to the city $327,200. The city's allocation was reduced by amounts allegedly spent by Marquette in its own land acquisitions. Net cost to government for a program whose principal purpose was the enhancement of Marquette was $10,744,001. Apparently, Marquette's only expenditure was $3,200,000 in credits for amounts the school claimed it had previously spent in acquiring land for itself in the area.

The net result of this arrangement, as with those in New York, St. Louis and Pittsburgh, was the enhancement at a highly strategic point of a religious institution. It is always argued of such arrangements that they serve the public interest since these institutions engage in the work of education. This is to a certain extent true. Yet unquestionably the church or its religious order is motivated in its operations by something deeper than education as a public service. It has a pervasive sectarian purpose in all its operations, its schools

160

particularly. Historically, the Catholic Canon Law at Canon 1374 forbade Catholics to attend not only public elementary schools but also public institutions of higher learning. They must in all cases, save where the local bishop for good reasons permitted exceptions, attend at all levels the schools of the church.[3] There can be no question as to the central role of higher education in the sectarian purposes of this church and the value of government subsidies of this kind in their fulfillment.

The Protestant commitment to higher education has been quite as consistent and quite as central to its religious purposes.

If the church is concerned only with the public purpose of educating youth, it can decisively demonstrate this by disassociating itself completely from the ownership and management of such an institution as Fordham or Marquette or St. Louis University. When the school is turned over to ownership and management of public agencies there can be no doubt as to the constitutionality and propriety of tax support.

Urban renewal has benefited many church organizations and institutions in many ways. We mention only a very few examples of the kind of church-state arrangement that is routinely fashioned in its operation. In Philadelphia St. Joseph College High School, a Jesuit institution, obtained land for a new parochial school and also $300,771 in federal funds to clear and develop the land. Total cost to the Jesuit order: $60,350. The University of Scranton, another institution of the Jesuit Fathers, used urban redevelopment procedures to oust 106 families and four commercial businesses from a site adjacent to its property and needed for its expansion. The area was in no sense a slum area but the renewal procedures were utilized on behalf of the church institution.

Baylor University of Waco, Texas, a Baptist institution, and Viterbo College of La Crosse, Wisconsin, and King's College of Wilkes Barre, Pennsylvania, both Catholic, have all utilized urban renewal for expansion purposes.

There have been other benefits to the churches in the urban renewal program. Renovation and construction funds have been provided for them under programs for renewing depressed areas. In Louisville, Kentucky, the Church of Our Merciful Saviour (Episcopal) obtained a government loan of $50,000 on the basis of

161

renewing substandard buildings in a renewal area. The loan was at three per cent for 20 years and was used to renovate the church, provide additional rooms, and modern plumbing and electrical wiring throughout. Broadway Temple A.M.E. Church also in the neighborhood put in for a $50,000 loan for similar purposes.

Urban renewal acquisition was utilized to provide a site for the multi-million dollar St. Mary's Catholic Cathedral in San Francisco. The land had already been sold to a developer for housing purposes. The Renewal Authority recalled the site, however, and directed that it be sold to the church.

One of the more bizarre chapters in the story of urban renewal was the attempt by a church to use it for the elimination of its competition. St. Coleman's Roman Catholic Church in Turtle Creek, near Pittsburgh, had located next door and almost under its eaves, the small Free Gospel Church. St. Coleman's needed the space to use as a playground in connection with its parish school. Its pastor sought repeatedly to buy the property. The congregation of the Free Gospel Church was happy with its location and did not wish to move. With many renewal programs going on in the Pittsburgh area, it occurred to the St. Coleman's pastor that he might use such a program to acquire the property and solve his troublesome problem.

It would have worked, too, save for a sharp public reaction which would not permit the deal to go through. On Dec. 3, 1964, an emotion-charged hearing was held by the County Commissioners. The meeting was crowded with indignant citizens who greeted the proposal with hostility. Charles C. Arensberg, Jr., an attorney representing the Free Gospel Church, declared: "This is the first time in the history of redevelopment in Pennsylvania that anyone has proposed taking property of one church for the benefit of another church." The following day Auxiliary Bishop Vincent M. Leonard announced that St. Coleman's would not take the land belongong to the Free Gospel Church.

Protestant groups also used urban renewal programs to their advantage. As a rule, however, they have been less astute politically than the Catholics and, on some projects at least, they have ended up paying more for less. A good example was the site of the old Germantown Academy in Philadelphia. The academy moved to the

162

suburbs and its old site was purchased in 1965 by the government's Redevelopment Authority for $975,000. There were two Protestant bidders for the land, both for the educational use that had been stipulated by the Authority. One was the Germantown Lutheran High School. The other was Germantown Friends School which was already operating in the area and wanted additional space for expansion. The competition became rather intense and this helps to explain why the government was able to receive from the eventual purchaser, Germantown Lutheran, the sum of $825,000. This was an unusually large return on such a resale where substantial markdowns are the rule. The competitive situation was eventually resolved by a decision to expand the project by another square block and to make part of the additional land available to Friends School. Also proposed was a plan to close a street, thus unifying and enlarging the Friends campus.

The Greek Orthodox Church of St. Nicholas was able to carry out a $500,000 expansion and renovation program in Newark, New Jersey, as a result of an urban renewal program. The church was permitted to buy at a greatly reduced price two acres of land adjacent to its existing facilities. The land was acquired for the church by the Newark Housing Authority.

In surplus government property Protestant organizations have done very well. In a report made in 1962 by Chester B. Lund, supervisor of federal surplus disposal, it was stated that Protestant churches had received real estate and buildings with an original value of $25,211,632 for which they paid only $133,227. A typical example is provided by Evangel College, an Assemblies of God institution located in Springfield, Missouri. The school was put into business by an original gift of 58.6 acres from the site of O'Reilly General Hospital in Springfield which had been declared surplus. Later, the same institution was able to arrange for the donation of an additional 29.95 acres by the Federal Government.

In its annual report of donations to churches for the fiscal year 1964, however, HEW showed that the Roman Catholic Church had received 41 per cent of the acreage going to religious groups. Most of this was obtained by the transfer of the Veterans Administration Hospital at Vancouver, Washington, to the Sisters of Charity of

Providence, a Catholic order. Second in total acreage donations was the Assemblies of God, a Protestant group.

The Seventh-day Adventists led in the number of donations received, 5 to 4 over the Catholics. The Adventists got no real estate, however, only "tool shed" donations with a top value of about $4,000. Other churches receiving real property donations were Baptist, Brethren, Lutheran, Church of Christ, Methodist, Christian and Independent. The donations to churches were much fewer in fiscal 1964 than in the previous years of the program, indicating that the post-war donations had about run out.

In 1966 the Federal Government donated to Church World Service (Protestant) $1 million worth of surplus property for the benefit of its overseas programs. The Agency for International Development paid the cost of ocean transportation while Church World Services paid for packing, crating and handling. The labeled surplus included various kinds of machinery and equipment. The surplus donation program so far as real estate and buildings are concerned is now relatively inactive. For the time being most of the domestic surplus has been given away.

As already indicated, the Catholics had their share of the give-aways. In 1964, St. Michael's College of Winooski, Vermont, obtained free of charge 116 acres and 14 buildings at the site of the Ethan Allen Air Force Base. The Federal Government declared surplus and conveyed to St. Mary's School (Catholic) of Shelby, Ohio, 18.4 acres. The school in this case paid 20 per cent of the fair value appraisal.

A case which aroused and sustained a bitter controversy involved disposal of 22 acres at Mitchel Field on Long Island. The record indicates that the Roman Catholic diocese of Rockville Centre had shown no interest in the land until it was brought to its attention by federal officials. When informed that the land was up for grabs, the diocese decided to put in a request. Also seeking 30 acres of the site for a religious school was the Hebrew Academy.

What made this case highly controversial was the fact that the East Meadow Public School District No. 3 had also made application for "suitable and necessary Mitchel Field acreage for educational (public school) purposes." Despite angry protests of a Citizens Mitchel Field Committee and a threatened lawsuit, the sales to the

164

two sectarian groups went through and they got the property at a 70 per cent discount. The usual discount in such sales was 80 per cent.

There are many other programs by which the Federal Government provides aid for church groups. Sometimes the government uses churches as distributors of food for the needy, both here and abroad. There have been a number of incidents involving the use of the distribution for proselytism. Hissom's Holiness Tabernacle in Charleston, West Virginia, handled distribution there along with two other churches. Rev. Earl G. Hissom, the pastor, regularly held a service and preached to the people who were coming to get their food. The Agricultural Marketing Service reacted swiftly to this situation when complaints were lodged.

In Santa Barbara County, California, the Roman Catholic Welfare Bureau handles distribution for the Federal Government. A similar program was planned for Fresno County where the Catholic Social Service sought to take over distribution from the County Board of Supervisors. A sharp community protest developed and the shift did not take place.

The same pattern can be observed in church distribution of food for the United States Government abroad. Church World Service (Protestant) and the Roman Catholic Relief Service have handled millions of pounds of food annually for distribution in many needy countries of the world. The use of religious groups for this program has been a constant source of dissatisfaction and complaint. The National Council of Churches became so disenchanted at one time that it served notice it would terminate its participation in this program. Eventually, it reconsidered.

The Catholic agency has handled the lion's share of the distribution in South Vietnam. It handled 106 million pounds of food in that one country alone during 1969. The choice of the church and clergy as distributors is defended with the logic that they are already on the scene, offering a convenient *modus operandi*. But it must be remembered that Catholics comprise at most only 10 per cent of that country's population — a militant minority. When they are administering the program it is inevitable that charges of proselytism in connection with the distribution will be constantly heard. Buddhist leaders do level such charges and also demand that they be desig-

165

nated for agents to distribute to Buddhists.

When this writer visited Vietnam in 1963, he particularly noted that nearly always the first complaint lodged by a Buddhist would relate to this issue. It seemed outrageous to Buddhists that the distribution of food should be monopolized by a religious minority which, according to them, used the distribution for proselytism. A second visit in 1971 disclosed that these issues were far from resolved.

On one occasion Frank Ellis, Food for Peace Director, actually denied the request of Catholic Relief for further distribution of food in Vietnam. The ruling was quickly changed, but here we have an indication of how a government official close to the scene actually felt about it. In the days of the Diem regime the food distribution became a scandal and brought an investigation with a report highly critical of Catholic Relief Services. The report was suppressed but word of it leaked out in Saigon and, eventually, to the United States. Perhaps one of the most criticized phases of the operation was Catholic administration of food to 150,000 members of the South Vietnamese militia. The food was included as part of their army pay.

Don Luce, writing in the *San Francisco Chronicle,* March 3, 1969, reported widespread dissatisfaction with the sectarian food distribution in South Vietnam. His judgment appeared to be that religion and relief were not mixing very well. Mr. Luce quoted Buddhist relief director Thich Nhat Thien as saying: "The Catholics give to the poor in order to undermine Buddhism and proselytize (for) Catholicism." Thich Nhat Thien was especially bitter over an episode which occurred following the great Tet offensive in 1968. According to him, he had been promised food for distribution to the people, but when he went to get it he was told that Buddhists would have to be supplied directly by Catholic Relief Services. He charged that the "Catholics do not want the Buddhists to control food distribution because then the Catholics would lose influence. They want the poor to turn to them so the poor will become Catholics."

In Latin America the writer has personally observed U.S. surplus openly on sale in the markets, though it was supposed to have been given away to the needy. He saw this so often and other observers have so frequently attested the same thing that this almost appears to be the characteristic outcome of the donation program.

How does this food regularly appear for sale in the markets? It is always possible, of course, that it has been donated to people who do not really need it. They sell it to regular distributors who place it in the markets. On the other hand, there are always suspicions that things are not right with the program in the first instance.

What the church-state partnership in food distribution does to the church is neatly illustrated by the statement of a priest in charge of distribution as quoted by the National Catholic News Service. Catholic Relief Services operating in Cochin, India, had been repeatedly charged with using the distribution of United States foods as a tool for proselytism. The irate priest in charge of the distribution exclaimed: "No. No. We have nothing to do with conversion. Our work is completely secular. There is nothing spiritual in it."[4]

Distribution of food through religious agents has an initial plausibility. It is humanitarian work which would appear appropriate to such groups. But so many doubts and problems have arisen in connection with church direction of food distribution that the wisdom of the entire method is now in question. Churches appear to value their sponsorship and management of such programs because of the prestige that accompanies them. But there are impressive disadvantages.

A related church-state problem in connection with foreign aid has been the use of foreign aid funds in the Agency for International Development and the Peace Corps to subsidize missionary movements abroad. A religious controversy erupted in 1964 when the magazine *Christianity Today* charged that the Peace Corps "exploits United States funds and personnel in a program of sectarian expansion."[5] *Christianity Today* charged specifically that in West Cameroon Roman Catholics had opened six new schools which they had staffed 100 per cent with U.S. Peace Corps personnel. A letter from R. Sargent Shriver, then head of the Peace Corps, acknowledged that Peace Corps personnel were indeed staffing the Catholic mission schools in West Cameroon, but argued that this had been the desire of the government there and that American officials had nothing to do with it. In any event the providing of funds for the maintenance of missionary operations and personnel abroad has been a frequent practice.

Yet another program of government financing which the churches have tapped for large gains is that of war damages and war claims. These grants made under the War Claims Act of 1948 and subsequent acts provided funds for the building of sectarian institutions in the Philippines. Here the rationale was that the money used was not really tax funds since it represented enemy assets confiscated by the United States at the outbreak of the war in 1941. Instead of returning the money to the erstwhile enemy owners, it should be used for good causes in the land where war damages had been suffered. Sponsor of the legislation for the benefit of the churches was Majority Leader of the House John McCormack, aided by a powerful lobby. The chief lobbyist was a Catholic layman, John A. O'Donnell, who collected 10 per cent of a total of $73 million for himself. Senator J. William Fulbright blew up when he heard of O'Donnell's activity and charged that the legislation had been passed by deception. This program of church aid resulted from a spate of bills, most of them rushed through in the waning moments of congressional sessions in the 1950s. By means of them, Rep. McCormack succeeded in providing some $30 million for Philippine churches which had a denominational counterpart in the United States. About $27 million of this went to the Roman Catholic Church and $3 million to assorted Protestant, Jewish and Baha'i groups. A prime example of the use of the funds was the construction of the Roman Catholic Cathedrals of Manila and Quezon City. As a result of grants to numerous institutions and dioceses, the Roman Catholic Church was able to establish an impressive institutional spread in the Philippines after World War II. For his essential role in the grants, Rep. McCormack was invested by the Pope with the rank of Knight Commander of the Order of St. Gregory the Great, with Star.

A form of association between churches and government which is now to be found in all our large cities is in housing programs — particularly housing for the elderly. Two programs in particular have proved attractive to churchmen: housing for the elderly built with FHA mortgage insurance, and similar housing financed by direct government loans from the Community Facilities Corporation. Seventy-five per cent of all the former kind of projects and over half the latter kind are now being undertaken in partnership between the Federal Government and the churches.

There is an ostensible propriety in this program. Is not housing for the elderly a kind of activity peculiarly appropriate to the churches? This has a humanitarian, a charitable ring that seems to put it in tune with the nature of the church. Church leaders have seemed to feel this, for they have rushed to the head of the line whenever government funding was available for such projects. But let us look more closely at these programs. What does the church itself get out of them?

The entire project which the sponsors propose is, of course, financed by the Federal Government via long-term, low-rate loans which the FHA or other funding agency guarantees. The elderly purchasers of apartments in the complex buy only a lifetime tenancy. This may cost them as much as $50,000. At their death ownership reverts to the corporation which sells the apartment again, and again, and again.

In one to two turnovers the church has recovered the initial investment. There is a tenant service charge of up to $400 a month as well. It is true that no individuals may profit personally from these projects since they are operated by nonprofit, tax-exempt corporations. (Often they enjoy real estate tax exemption as well.) But once the profits start rolling in, the church can use them to finance other housing projects or to add improvements to the original. The profits may also be plowed into the church's own program, providing a continuing endowment.

The church itself may directly build, own and manage the property, or it may set up a related corporation for this purpose. Note the case of St. John's Towers, Stamford, Connecticut. This handsome complex comprises three 17-story middle income apartments with 352 units. It is owned by the Roman Catholic diocese of Bridgeport.

In Jackson, Mississippi, the Roman Catholic diocese of Natchez-Jackson has received a "firm commitment" for a low-cost housing project of 100 units. The government will guarantee the mortgage and also supplement rentals for those unable to pay. The diocese will be in charge and would presumably enjoy whatever profits are to be realized from the project.

An interesting Catholic project in retirement housing is the high rise planned by the San Diego diocese in that city. Cathedral Girls High School was closed because of lack of patronage and the high rise to cost $2.5 million will replace it. The project will be financed by a long-term, low-interest loan by the Department of Housing and Urban Development.

Note, also, the Friendship Terrace project of Washington, D.C. This is an Episcopal Church Home financed by a federal loan of $2,790,000 from the U.S. Department of Housing and Urban Development.

In lowcost housing programs, the risk to the church is, again, minimal, since the government guarantees the loans and often pays the rents as well. All of this continues to create both the image and substance of a church-state combine — a kind of religio-political operation for people service. Such endeavors are undertaken with motives and purposes that are ostensibly good. They will provide education, food, health care, housing, welfare for the people. But these operations are all supported by tax funds collected under compulsion from all the people. What is widely overlooked is that along with the service rendered the structure of the church is sustained. The taxpayers are not only paying for the service, they are also paying for the church. They are paying for it under attractive guises and to the accompaniment of pleasant sounds, but they are paying for it all the same.

Whatever the particular arrangement by which state and church team up in housing projects, it is certainly not separation of church and state. Is this some new and beneficient program which will work for the welfare of society? Or is it a new version of an arrangement that has brought grief and misery to mankind?

Sometimes the church sets up an independent corporate entity to engage in the housing business. The entity so created is typically directed by a board of trustees composed of its own votaries which operates in the name of the church or in a closely related name. For example, there is Baptist Terrace Apartments in Orlando, Florida, a project with 197 apartments.[6] It is sponsored by First Baptist Housing, Inc., a nonprofit organization composed exclusively of members of the First Baptist Church of Orlando. Another church retirement home in Orlando is Orlando Central Towers with 198 apartments, sponsored by the Central Nazarene Church of Orlando, whose house of worship immediately adjoins the project. Still another is Kinneret with 168 apartments sponsored by the Central Florida Jewish Community Council.

All three of these large projects were financed by the Federal Department of Housing and urban Development. The loans were for 50 years with interest at 3 per cent. All three projects have waiting lists. The operators insisted that the policy of admissions was on a nonsectarian, nondiscriminatory basis as required by the Federal Government. But the affinity between church and state was evidentally close and continuing.

Consider the Presbyterian Community Apartments, a 16-story high-rise in Fort Myers, Florida. This building would return $57,000 annually to the community in taxes, but it is exempt from tax. The building was financed by the federal government with a $2 million loan at 3 per cent over 50 years. It is a HUD project which stipulates that single tenants may have no more than $4,860 in annual income. But there are reports that many of the tenants have a much larger income. A special provision of Florida law exempts such church projects from tax.

Episcopal Retirement Homes, Inc. of California is a corporation which developed from St. Paul's Episcopal Church. The Rev. Darby Betts is rector of St. Paul's Church and president of Episcopal Homes, Inc., which has two large projects of retirement housing — St. Paul's Towers and Canterbury Woods. Mr. Betts receives salaries from both church and corporation and the church receives rental from Episcopal Homes, Inc. for office space in its parish hall. Both the church and the retirement homes are exempt from real estate tax. The tenant pays an entry fee of $12,500 to $47,000 which purchases only a life tenancy in an apartment. In addition he pays a monthly rental of $200 to $365. It would appear that Episcopal Retirement Homes, Inc. could recover the complete investment in one turnover. It could use subsequent income to build another complex or as a continuing endowment for St. Paul's Church.

Nor did these two immense projects exhaust the potential of Episcopal federal housing programs in the San Francisco bay area. Lester Kinsolving of the *San Francisco Chronicle*, who has written in

171

detail of these projects, describes yet another apartment house complex for the elderly which the San Francisco Episcopal diocese is contemplating.[7] The complex is planned as a device to shore up the declining finances of the diocese.

Again, we must look at the composite picture. Taken by itself, each of the programs described above can offer a plausible rationale. But taken together, they point inexorably to those reciprocal embroilments which the Supreme Court insisted it was the purpose of the First Amendment to avoid. Here are a multitude of schemes in which government finances church programs with interlocking of management between the two. The composite picture is that of an establishment of religion. For here we see the church spreading its institutions far and wide across the land with the promotional and financial power of the state. Whether it is the recipient of government donations or subsidies, the agent of government in the use or distribution of surplus property and food, the beneficiary of government power of eminent domain, or the partner of government in housing, medicine or education, the church inevitably lands in this kind of involvement. It is certain that this is not separation of church and state. It is equally certain that this condition is not healthy for either church or state.

NOTES

1. Larson, Martin A. and Lowell, C. Stanley, *Praise the Lord for Tax Exemption*, Robert B. Luce, Inc., Washington, D.C., 1969, p.244

2. For a complete discussion of these rules, see Healy, Edwin F., S.J., *Medical Ethics*, Loyola University Press, 1956

3. Bouscaren, T. Lincoln and Ellis, Adam C., *Canon Law, a Text and Commentary*, Third Revised Edition, 1957, Bruce, Milwaukee, p.744

4. *Christianity Today*, April 10, 1970

5. *Christianity Today*, August 28, 1964

6. For a helpful discussion of this and the following projects, see the *Christian Science Monitor*, April 10, 1970

7. *San Francisco Chronicle*, June 22, 1968

8.   The Church Opportunity Act

From time immemorial the church has been concerned with poverty. Relief of the poor has always been considered one of the primary tasks of the church. Indeed, churches, voluntary societies and beneficent individuals were operating in the anti-poverty field long before the state entered it. In the United States, government did not really get into the business of poverty relief on any significant scale until the New Deal of the 1930's. The New Deal came with a shout, calling the nation publicly and clamantly to dedicate its resources to the relief of the underprivileged. It was at this time that the attack on poverty became a prime activity of government with its own administrative apparatus and vast expenditures to sustain it.

Church operations in the anti-poverty field have in the past been simple, direct and personal. They were also voluntary, Funds were contributed by those who could afford to give. These funds were received by church authorities and duly expended by them for relief of the poor. There was no official coercion, no taxation. No government authority was even remotely involved in such activity. The church was doing its own thing. It was doing what came naturally. It was doing what it would have been difficult or impossible not to do. Relief of the poor was its own chosen act.

In the massive anti-poverty programs of the New Deal the church was not involved at all. Apparently no one even suggested it. Save for possible pulpit encouragement to continue its good work, government was alone in this endeavor. Its programs were conceived and administered by public officials and paid for with public funds.

In 1964 a new concept of anti-poverty effort emerged. This concept joined state and church in a functional arrangement. It crept in stealthily, without fanfare. Only a few arch manipulators had any real notion of what was taking place. The new concept emerged and was written into law without any great public debate. The whole nature of church-state relations in the United States was drastically shifted with hardly anybody knowing about it.

The Economic Opportunity Act of 1964 was passed and in operation before there was any general recognition that it brought church and state together in a kind of partnership previously unknown in this country. Under this legislation churches have been major beneficiaries of government and are now administratively involved with the state in carrying on all kinds of anti-poverty programs. The anti-poverty bill was passed in the spirit of a great crusade. The conquest of poverty had been a big plank in the Democratic platform for the elections of 1960 and 1962. President Johnson signed the bill amid wide acclaim.

What may yet turn out to have been the most significant feature of this legislation received relatively little attention. The reference is to the church-state issue which in the studied nebulousness of the Economic Opportunity Act was almost entirely obscured. The Act was composed of broad generalities which enabled it to spill over into an amazing conglomerate of activities and programs in widely divergent fields. In the thick of the thing from start to finish were the clerical operators, on the one hand, and their co-conspirators among the legislators, on the other. Both were eager to bring state and church into partnership in the anti-poverty enterprise. Churchmen saw in the proposed legislation myriad opportunities to obtain the money and prestige of government for their own operations. Certain legislators saw a chance to utilize the clerical structure to administer government programs and also to win political support.

The clerical opportunists were, in fact, looking far beyond the poverty programs to other forms of government aid for which they thought these might serve as precedent. If churches could function as agents of government in anti-poverty programs, then why not in education programs? Why not in any kind of federal programs whatever? Roman Catholic Bishop William E. McManus saw this clearly when he pointed out in an address to the Ohio Catholic Education Association on September 23, 1965 that while benefits to the church from the Economic Opportunity Act had not been large, its significance lay in the fact that it had marked "the beginning of a national policy which requires the equitable distribution of federal aid to all school children."

If we substitute "all schools" for "all school children" we have his real meaning. The hiring of churches for anti-poverty programs would provide the precedent for hiring churches for education activities as well. Indeed, once this kind of operation got under way who could say what was anti-poverty and what was educational or other? Was it not all one vast program of human uplift in which church and state would join, a great effort for the good of mankind? In this new partnership the church would call the tune and the state would pay the piper. At least that is what the churchmen hoped.

What, then, of the great nation-wide debate as the legislators pondered this historic reversal? Were defenders of constitutional separation of church and state arrayed in the public forum against protagonists of a new clericalism in a Webster-Hayne confrontation? Nothing of the kind happened. Never before in the history of political thought has so monumental a change been effected by so few in such complete darkness. It is possible that even some of the principal participants in the scene scarcely understood what it was all about. Yet they were actually making a monumental change in the basic church-state pattern under which the nation had operated for a century and a half.

The issue was fought out almost solely in the privacy of Congressional committees and the relative privacy of their hearings attended by a score of churchmen, social workers and educators. Through it all, the churchmen evidenced one overpowering concern — to cut the church into the bill, to set up a precedent for a widening government subsidy to church programs. Their strategy was to keep the language so vague that there would be plenty of openings for the church to slip in.

Viewed in this perspective, it will be seen that the OEO (Office of Economic Opportunity, 1964) foreshadowed the ESEA (Elementary and Secondary Education Act, 1965). A few leaders did see where the proposals were pointing in church-state relations and fought them bitterly. But the clerical leaders and their political coterie were more than a match for them. Realizing that the church-state problems in the two bills were identical, Rep. James Delaney, an intimate of the late Cardinal Spellman and a member of the strategic House Rules Committee, insisted he would vote against a "rule" for any anti-poverty bill unless it was "cleared" by his co-religionist and Brooklyn colleague, Rep. Hugh Carey of the Education Committee. In practical logistics this meant that there would be no anti-poverty bill passed unless the committee agreed to put in it something that could be used later as a precedent to get federal aid for Catholic schools.

A letter to President Johnson at the time this controversy was boiling behind the scenes produced a letter from his aide, Brooks Hays, dated March 16, 1964:

> The President . . . would not recommend the inclusion of private or parochial schools because this would violate the Constitutional provisions with reference to separation of church and state. He hopes that in poverty situations some special aids, which do not pertain to religious instructions, for health and nutrition of individual children may be authorized without infringing upon the Constitution.

Because of the looseness with which the law was drawn, churches were eventually able to receive direct aid from government in ways not possible under other laws. There are two provisions of the law — Section 203 and Section 113 — which have opened the door for church aid. Neither makes any mention of churches, but the door was left ajar and they have rushed in. Section 203 authorizes grants for anti-poverty purposes to "private, nonpublic organizations to pay all or part of the costs of development of community action programs." This was an open invitation to the churches to operate in the welfare field with government money.

Section 113 of the Economic Opportunity Act provides that both federal funds and the labor of federal enrollees may be used for "local projects sponsored by private, nonprofit organizations." This provision made possible the use of federal funds for the purchase, construction and maintenance of church buildings to house antipoverty programs. The nature of these programs was left extremely vague. Local groups were invited to come up with ideas. Certainly church programs in which religious proselytism was mingled with poverty relief became an immediate possibility. How could a determination be made as to what was charitable and what was religious?

To be sure, the law does contain the "sectarian disclaimer" which has become almost a standard feature of church aid legislation. It follows the description of projects that may be financed with federal funds with this qualification: "other than projects involving the construction, operation or maintenance of any facility used or to be used for sectarian instruction or as a place of worship." The law thus bars use of the funds for construction and maintenance of houses of worship or to finance programs of sectarian instruction. But within the broad latitude of programs conceived and designed in one way or another to relieve poverty there was wide room for church subsidy.

Parish buildings not specifically designed for worship and the antipoverty programs in them could be financed by government. The churches have, in fact, been quick to seize the opportunities under this legislation. They have been prime beneficiaries of the Economic Opportunity Act, shifting the costs of their charitable and welfare programs to government and adding other programs at government expense. Even the costs of their houses of worship have occasionally been assumed by the Federal Government under this legislation. This, despite the sectarian disclaimer.

There has been another rather astonishing involvement of church with state under the antipoverty program. This is the mass shift of personnel from pulpit to government office. Literally thousands of Protestant ministers and Roman Catholic priests and nuns have left their positions with the church in order to become administrators of antipoverty programs. R. Sargent Shriver, chief of the OEO, once commented on this. He said that so many of the clergy had gone to work for OEO that the initials had taken on a new meaning. He said: "OEO now means Office of Ecclesiastical Outcasts!" The remark of the Rev. Michael F. Kennelly, S.J., is interesting. As he succeeded another priest as director of the federal Program Innovation in health care, he remarked: "I turn now to a new work — health care for the poor. I pray that I can render a significant service in this important field." (*Religious News Service*, July 22, 1970).

The distribution of government funds to the churches for antipoverty programs has become standard procedure in many communities. So much so that the funding of projects is often referred to as the parish list. Church representatives simply get together and divide up the available funds. While serving as head of OEO, R. Sargent Shriver addressed the Diamond Jubilee banquet of the Sisters of the Blessed Sacrament. On that occasion he presented a government check for $7.5 million to the Roman Catholic diocese of Natchez-Hattiesburg for its antipoverty programs in the State of Mississippi. He remarked:

> Three or four years ago it was impossible for a federal agency to give a direct grant to a religious group. Today we are giving hundreds of grants without violating the principle of separation of church and state.[2]

From the very start, churches were prominent in asking and receiving the federal allocations. A large grant in 1964 — $1,399,509 — went to the New Mexico Council of Churches for its program among migrant workers. It is safe to say that the amounts received from government exceeded by several times the amounts received by the Council from other sources. One of the strengths of its application lay in the fact that this Council includes both the Protestant bodies of New Mexico and the Roman Catholic diocese of

Santa Fe. In neighboring Arizona the Protestant Council of Churches received grants through 1969 of $2,326,817 for its programs. Another Protestant Council of Churches, that of North Carolina, received a federal grant of $270,444 for its program among migrants. On a national basis, 5 of 26 of the initial grants for work among migrants were awarded to churches. Once such programs are established the disposition is to renew their funds.

A report issued by the OEO in 1966 shows the grants for Head Start programs in New York City. Among these are many grants to churches.

Brooklyn Catholic Schools	$571,199
Cardinal Spellman Center	15,477
Church of the Good Shepherd	18,410
Elizabeth Seton League	23,571
Church of God in Christ	13,906
Jewish Foundation School	26,375
New York City Mission Society	8,559
Northeast Conference of Seventh-day Adventists	49,102
Rabbi Jacob Joseph School	8,557
St. Augustine's Episcopal School	49,423
St. Theresa's Church	15,079
Sharon Baptist Church	15,721
Temple of God Missionary Baptist Church	10,385
Van Alst Methodist Church	8,704
Victory Baptist Church	18,706
Yeshiva Day School	15,843

Catholic Head Start programs in 1965 in Washington, D.C., started off with a Mass for all participants. Seton Hill College and St. Vincent College (Catholic), Jeanette, Pennsylvania, received in 1966 $60,018 for work-study programs; also $261,600 for work experience programs involving 320 participants; and basic education grants totaling $22,240. These small schools received numerous other forms of federal aid as well.

The Pacoima (California) Congregational Church received an OEO grant of $242,316 for a project with unemployed youth. The program, it was said, was designed to build a bridge between the community and various agencies. The Roman Catholic diocese of Buffalo, New York, received among various grants one for $65,278

179

for summer education programs. A grant of $191,572 was made to the Detroit archdiocese to improve school services. The New Orleans archdiocese received over $400,000 in initial grants for its programs. The Zion Hill Missionary Baptist Church of Contra Costa County, California, received a grant for a summer work-study program with youth.

In Chicago the "parish list" for fiscal 1967 included the following:

Roman Catholic	$1,040,377
Episcopal Diocese	34,285
First Presbyterian Church	63,785
Greater M.E. Church	48,710
Great St. John A.M.E. Church	59,789
Ecumenical Council	130,000
Chicago Council on Religion & Race	201,803
Total	$1,577,749

Following are a few typical instances picked at random from thousands. In Detroit, programs in seven Roman Catholic schools drew an allocation of $191,572; in New Haven, Connecticut, one such institution was granted $29,810. In Baton Rouge, Louisiana, the Roman Catholic diocese got control of the antipoverty program as it did in Lake Charles. The initial Head Start programs in Puerto Rico brought a grant of $627,780 which was shared by the Second Baptist Church, Hato Rey; United Presbyterian Church, San Juan; and the Evangelical Council of Puerto Rico. In Cleveland, Ohio, Head Start got underway with an initial grant of $815,237. The program reached six Catholic schools and 18 Protestant churches, in addition to 61 public schools. Sponsors included the Cleveland archdiocese and the Greater Cleveland Council of Churches. The First Methodist Church of Danbury, Connecticut, housed Head Start there. The initial grant: $38,418 with a follow-up allocation of $6,142.

The Hancock County (Ohio) Council of Churches administered a $16,714 federal program. Nine thousand, seven hundred and forty-six dollars was allocated to the Wyoming Valley (Pennsylvania) Council of Churches for a tri-county program for migrants.

Churches participated either by receiving the funds in direct grants, or by receiving them as delegate agencies of a Community Action Agency.

In thousands of instances across the country, church and state joined in the Head Start programs. The tie-ups were many. The church was paid a rental for its facilities which varied greatly but in some instances was sufficient to save it from mortgage foreclosure. Church personnel clad in religious regalia were frequently the paid leaders and teachers, and religious images and indicia adorned the walls. Management was supposedly exercised by an independent community organization, but in many situations this was simply an alter ego of the church. Then there was always the hope, as one minister put it, that there might be "the possibility of getting parents some day to attend our church." The holding of so many of the neighborhood programs in churches made it mandatory upon parents to send their children into religious buildings if they wished to participate.

An antipoverty program at First English Lutheran Church, Columbus, Ohio, was initiated by the church but was eventually funded with an OEO grant of $185,000. In Worcester, Massachusetts, Catholic Charities, an arm of the Catholic diocese, was chosen to operate a center of services to help the poor improve their lot. The *Catholic Standard and Times,* official publication of the Philadelphia archdiocese, contained in its issue of July 5, 1968, a summary of its welfare programs financed by the Federal Government. These include Operation Discovery, Operation Overbrook, Operation Outbound, Newman Camperships, Contact, Ravenhill Day Camp, S.A.I.L., Pope John Centers, R.S.V.P., Operation Manna, and the S.H.A.L.O.M. Day Camp. Grants to maintain these projects ran to at least $505,080. For comparable programs the Pittsburgh diocese received $435,690.

One of the features of the Economic Opportunity Act which created frictions and resentments was the provision of federal funds to pay the salaries of church personnel presumably engaged in antipoverty endeavors. Such personnel were often put to work for religious institutions, performing secretarial duties, maintaining grounds, repairing and adding to buildings. At Evansville, Indiana,

181

the staffs of Catholic parochial schools were augmented by personnel reimbursed by the federal antipoverty program. In Evansville-Vanderburgh County, 183 persons received employment during the school year of 1964-65 and 62 through the summer months. Of these, 138 and 21, respectively, were employed in the parochial schools. Rev. James Deneen, diocesan superintendent of schools and head of the mayor's personnel committee, acknowledged the great lift this had given to the diocesan program. He explained that only two of the parochial schools had been able to afford a secretary on the staff until the inauguration of this federal program.

Nazareth College of Rochester, New York, an institution of the Sisters of St. Joseph, received $4,140 in federal antipoverty funds to provide for additional help at the school ranging from clerk and typist to dormitory and library assistants. In Denver, Colorado, $67,850 was allocated for 265 jobs in six Catholic high schools. Despite strong protests on constitutional grounds, the arrangement stood.

In Washington, D.C., our Lady of Perpetual Help Church used the antipoverty program to make substantial improvements on its property. The church added a brick retaining wall and improved and beautified its grounds. A story in the *Washington Evening Star,* July 30, 1967, quoted charges made by Nadine Winters of Hospitality House that "Some ministers have a racket going." She asserted that clergymen were collecting funds from the Office of Economic Opportunity for the use of buildings, additional funds for projects, and even added members to their regular staffs with salaries paid from the same source. Dr. Herman Tyrance, director of the Washington, D.C. programs commented: "The use of public money for religious institutions is wrong, without question."

A Fall, 1965 OEO report on activities of the Job Corps said that corpsmen at the Schenck (Pisgah Forest, N.E.) Center spent Saturday afternoons "repairing the Sacred Heart Church in Brevard." In Jacksonville, Florida, The Greater Jacksonville Economic Opportunity, Inc. had its offices in the parish house of the Immaculate Conception Roman Catholic Church.

In the operations of the OEO certain religious orders of the Roman Catholic Church have been able to broaden greatly a program of public assistance which they had been carrying on for many years. This involves the hiring out of religious personnel to government for the performance of services which are labeled public but really enhance the church itself. A survey made back in 1958 by Americans United indicated that at least 2,000 nuns were then serving as public school teachers in at least 18 states. Others served as postal employees and government workers of various kinds. Members of religious orders also serve as chaplains in the armed services. If these persons are members of a religious order under a vow of poverty, their entire salary, without any withholding or social security, goes to their order. The order provides the nun or priest with a subsistence stipend and pockets the rest. This becomes, in effect, a kind of public donation to the church.

Citizens of Boston were amazed over a disclosure of such a situation involving a Franciscan nun, Sister Francis Georgia Vincents of South Boston, whose story was told in the *Herald Traveler,* Feb. 25, 1970. The newspaper story revealed that this Sister was working for city hall for $1,000 a year to cover her expenses while her $6,500 salary was paid without tax to her order. This procedure rarely gets publicity but it has become commonplace in the OEO. Because the employee is under a vow of poverty and is presumed, therefore, to have nothing, his salary can be, and usually is, paid over to the church which profits handsomely from the arrangement.

Many parochial schools and church-related colleges augmented their work crews and paid them with federal funds. Such practices by the Philadelphia archdiocese drew the protests of the Greater Philadelphia Council of Churches, the Episcopal Diocese of Pennsylvania, and Lutheran, Methodist, Baptist and United Church of Christ leaders, as well as the American Civil Liberties Union, the Philadelphia Teachers Association, the Philadelphia Home and School Council, and Jewish organizations. Spencer Coxe, executive director of the Philldelphia ACLU said that he did not object to the practice of paying personnel at sectarian orphanages, hospitals and retirement homes with government funds. "But," he said, "Catholic schools . . . are sectarian institutions and they have a specifically religious purpose, to provide religious instruction and to indoctrinate Catholic children. This is a perfectly proper purpose, but not one the government should support."[3] The programs went right on just the same.

The *Catholic Standard*, December 1, 1966, reported that "nearly 240,000 persons . . . have been enrolled or served by antipoverty programs conducted at more than 2,300 Catholic facilities. . . ." The report also asserted that Catholic sources had enlisted the directors of the programs a few of which were Head Start, Neighborhood Youth Corps, Upward Bound, Work-Study, work training, basic education for adults, and remedial education. The report denied that there was any proselytizing in connection with the programs.

There were grim struggles for control of local OEO programs and the money that went with them. Sometimes the churches were involved. An alleged Catholic take-over of the antipoverty program in San Antonio, Texas, was too much for the Rev. Gerald McAllister, canon of a local Episcopal Church. Canon McAllister specifically charged that James Kazen, an agent for the Roman Catholic archdiocese, had rigged the election to the Economic Opportunities Development Corporation which was to direct the San Antonio projects.[4] At stake in the controversy was control of one of the south's largest antipoverty programs. Said Canon McAllister in quoting some of his Mexican-American friends: "Our memory in Mexico goes back to a time when this pattern dominated the life of our nation. We do not want it here."

Sometimes it was just a case of being unable to resist the sudden influx of federal largesse. So the Rev. Willie Johnson, pastor of Bronx Evangelistic Church, New York City, went on trial accused of living in high style on antipoverty grants, of paying exorbitant salaries to himself, his parents and his sister, and remodeling their apartment with funds allocated for programs.

Another prime source of inter-creedal friction was the use of religious personnel clad in religious garb as leaders of the program as well as buildings adorned with religious images and indicia. This was done in numerous situations despite the provision set forth in Section Six of the *Conditions Applicable to the Use of Grants for Activities to Be Conducted by a Church or Church-Related*

Organization: "Facilities renovated or rented for programs financed in whole or in part by this grant shall be devoid of sectarian or religious symbols, decorations, or other sectarian identification."

Church symbols frequently remained in place, however. Occasionally, there was a protest of the kind lodged by the First Baptist Church of Johns Island, South Carolina, objecting to sectarian conduct of the migrant project at Haut Gap School. The protest charged that Roman Catholic sisters wearing religious garb were drawing federal salaries for their work at the project. This, the church claimed, violated the OEO conditions.

The *Washington Post* editorialized on August 18, 1965:

> (The church-state problem) is not obviated . . . by the stipulation in the antipoverty programs that projects using church facilities must be open to persons of all faiths, that religious instruction may not be given, and that religious symbols must be covered up. Churches are commonly open to persons of all faiths; that is . . . how they proselyte. And no amount of covering up of religious symbols can avoid making the religious institution itself seem the source of benefactions financed out of public funds. For all the good intentions and good will entailed, we believe there is more danger than welfare in this partnership between church and state.

The *New York Times,* May 24, 1965, also expressed the view that the Head Start programs under OEO were ignoring constitutional separation of church and state and should be tested in the court. The *Times* pointed to the fact that in the New York program the New York and Brooklyn Roman Catholic dioceses together were to get over $440,000, an amount which should be compared with the $2.6 million to go to the city's Board of Education. The Methodist Church was scheduled for $75,342 and other churches were included. The *Times* editorial drew this reaction from the constitutional lawyer Leo Pfeffer:

> Involvement of church-related institutions in Project Head Start and other antipoverty programs constitutes a major step backward. Because of the church's traditional prominence in the field of charity, those who enter a church building to avail themselves of the benefits of the project will again experience

185

the degrading feeling of being a recipient of charity. . . .

What is doubly disturbing about the situation is that it is basically dishonest. During the centuries that the church dispensed alms it was expending funds voluntarily contributed to it by the faithful. Under the Government's antipoverty program it is expending tax funds raised through compulsion of law. Project Head Start requires the church to contribute only 10 per cent of the cost, and even this is fictional, since the contribution may be made in kind, including the rental value for use of the church premises.[5]

The Economic Opportunity Act has not only been used to combine church and government operations. It has also been used to undermine the public school system through the promotion and financing of private and sectarian schools. The plan to divert public funds from public to private and sectarian schools has been presented under the guise of promoting competition in education. The Nixon Administration itself was said to favor development of tuition voucher programs as a means of providing federal aid to parochial schools. Certainly it had approved initial grants for experiments with such programs.

The tuition voucher program was said to foster competition by dividing the educational funds with parochial schools. This was to be done by offering parents of school children a tuition grant which would be receivable for their child's tuition in any school where they might wish to send him and where he could obtain admission.

The tuition voucher proposal is not new. It was proposed by a Jesuit professor at Marquette University, the Rev. Virgil A. Blum, more than 20 years ago. He conceived and advocated the plan as a means of circumventing the constitutional ban on government aid to religious schools. The idea was that if the government money would pause a moment with the parent, at least theoretically, before going to the school, this would ease the constitutional problem. Even before Blum, a program of this kind was actually in operation in Vermont. As we noted in Chapter 6 however, the Vermont Supreme Court found the plan in violation of the First and Fourteenth Amendments and the United States Supreme Court did not choose to review the case.

It is, nevertheless, this very tuition voucher program which OEO has decided to push. Why the OEO rather than the Office of Education? At first blush, there seems to be no logic whatever in the implementation of such a scheme with federal, antipoverty funds. The explanation lies in the loose provisions of the Economic Opportunity Act which have made possible a weird assortment of vagaries. An initial grant by OEO provided $196,313 to Christopher Jencks at the Center for the Study of Public Policy, Cambridge, Massachusetts. A study was made of the feasibility of the tuition voucher proposal. A study of the Jencks report would seem to indicate that a considerable part of the grant must have gone to lawyers as fees for trying to figure ways the tuition voucher plan could get around the constitutional ban on aid to religious institutions. As might have been predicted, Jencks reported that the proposal was feasible and highly desirable. The plan he offered envisaged additional grants of $40 million for pilot projects in a series of communities through the nation. Parochial schools would receive a $600 annual tuition grant for each child whose parents chose that institution and were able to get him admitted. If the parents chose a public school, that school would receive only the difference between that figure and the average per-child expenditure already being paid in public schools.

Implementation of the tuition voucher proposals on a wide scale would undermine the public schools as institutions of excellence, tending to leave them as the dumping ground for private school rejects. The plain fact is that many parents today are fearful. They would willingly pull out their children from the common schools and leave those schools to rot, except for one reason. They cannot afford it. But suppose that government were to supply the money. Suppose government would agree to pay tuition in a church school or other private school for every student who can gain admission there. The best of the students would promptly desert the common schools, leaving in them only the under-average and the misfits who could not gain admiision to private schools. Thus, the public schools which must take all and exclude none, would collapse into mediocrity and worse, and we should become a nation of predominantly private schools with a public system for the poor. This is exactly what our

187

free, democratic concepts have always sought to avoid. One can hardly imagine an outcome more damaging to national unity and to democratic institutions.

How would the United States Supreme Court view the tuition voucher plan? We have already discussed this matter in Chapter 6. If tuition voucher proposals are implemented, we shall undoubtedly see the plan subjected to a constitutional test in the High Court.

The OEO is being tapped by many church-related institutions as another source of funds to carry their administrative overhead. Consider the program called Upward Bound. Here funds are provided to a college for the purpose of recruiting summer students presumably from low income groups. For 50 students little College of St. Mary of the Springs, a Roman Catholic school, received $65,559. The total enrollment of the college was listed as just over 400. It appears that this grant would carry a respectable share of the school's annual budget. The same would likely be true of little Mars Hill Baptist College of North Carolina which in 1968 drew $66,609 to finance an Upward Bound program for 50 students.

An examination of the OEO reports shows many such allocations to sectarian institutions; Brandeis University (Jewish) $122,627 for 80 students; Barat College of the Sacred Heart (Catholic) $195,000 for 150 students; Baldwin-Wallace (Methodist) $78,566 for 75 students; St. Mary's University (Catholic) $65,650 for 50 students; Virginia Union University (Baptist) $120,390 for 130 students; Alaska Methodist University $118,185 for 60 students; Spring Hill College (Catholic) $77,218 for 50 students; Bloomfield College (Presbyterian) $30,000 for 50 students; and many, many others.

But this is not all. There are supplemental grants to be obtained. These are available to the same schools for "follow up" programs. Many of these, the record shows, come back in for additional grants and receive them. All of these expenditures are for the laudable purpose of interesting young people in a college education. But one of the important side effects is to provide government aid for the administrative costs of church schools.

Many of the programs being carried on under the Economic

Opportunity Act appeared to be unconstitutional on church-state grounds. Often they involved direct payments by government to the churches. How could these escape identification as acts respecting establishment of religion? In practice, however, the whole anti-poverty program has appeared remarkably elusive so far as lawsuits are concerned. The kind of difficulties encountered can be illustrated by the effort of Americans United to bring a definitive court test of the church-state involvements in a Kansas City OEO program. The organization together with 18 local taxpayer-plaintiffs decided to challenge a particularly overt case of sectarian favoritism in a Head Start program.

The plaintiffs stated that their purpose was not to oppose the Kansas City project "but only to insure that it is administered solely by public agencies, and not by private, religious agencies." The Kansas City program was particularly bad from the church-state point of view because public sponsors and buildings had been cavalierly passed over in favor of sectarian operators. Actually, the public school board was ready to take on administration of all the projects and there were public facilities available for the programs in every neighborhood. The suit charged that the proposed participation by the Roman Catholic diocese aids religion because it causes a public welfare program to be conducted by religious institutions. It places behind such participation the power, prestige and financial support of governmental bodies. It causes a fusion of governmental and religious functions. It causes tax money to be used in support of a religious activity or institution. It furnishes tax funds to parochial schools.

Government officials issued statements saying that they welcomed the suit and were glad to have the church-state issue tested in court. Then they quietly shifted this particular program to public management and public facilities. Thus, the case became moot since the ground of the complaint had been dissolved. There has actually been no definitive court test of the various forms of church aid which have characterized the operation of the Economic Opportunity Act. Apparently, only the reduction of antipoverty funds and programs will dissolve the church-state ties fostered by this federal legislation.

By its very ambiguities the Economic Opportunity Act has

invited the sectarian involvements and abuse which have characterized it from the start. The OEO has, in effect, taken on more and more of the financing of church welfare programs. This has quite changed the church's role in this field from bold innovator to government chore boy. The church's welfare administration becomes a part of the government bureaucracy with the result that we have long learned to anticipate. The church abandons its creative role and locks itself into routine for the sake of a pay check.

Notes

1. *World Outlook*. April, 1968
2. *Catholic Standard*. February 17, 1966
3. *Philadelphia Inquirer*. February 6, 1966
4. *San Antonio News*. May 13, 1966
5. The New York Times, *June 18, 1965*

9. Where Are We Going in Church and State?

Before we look at where we are going let us look at where we have been. For the past century-and-a-half the church-state pattern in the United States is one which has been generally and familiarly described as separation of church and state. Within a decade after the adoption of the First Amendment, Thomas Jefferson wrote to the Danbury Baptist Association as follows:

> Believing with you that religion is a matter which lies solely between man and his God, that he owes account to none other for his faith or his worship, that the legislative powers of government reach actions only, and not opinions, I contemplate with sovereign reverence that act of the whole American people which declared that their legislature should "make no law respecting an establishment of religion, or prohibiting the free exercise thereof," thus building a wall of separation between church and state.[1]

The statement of Jefferson was deliberate. He had planned it carefully and put into it exactly what he meant to convey. He thought of the American arrangement as one which relegated religion altogether to the realm of free choice. Religion was to be entirely volitional, divorced forever from the coercive power of the state. The formal and official separation of church and state was but symbolic of the deeper separation which meant that men were never to be coerced in the realm of religion. The religious enterprise was to

191

be entirely on its own. It would have from the state nothing but freedom — freedom to produce whatever it could produce. If it failed to produce anything, if it could not on its own attract adherents and support, it would just have to die.

The separation between church and state was to apply at the money line. This was basic to the entire arrangement as the prolonged debates both over the Virginia Bill for Establishing Religious Freedom and the First Amendment itself make clear. The thinking of at least some of the Founders about church financing was disclosed in this classic from Benjamin Franklin:

> When a religion is good . . . it will support itself and when it cannot support itself and God does not care to support it, so that professors are obliged to call for help of the civil power, it is the sign . . . of its being a bad one.[2]

Examine the language of the religion clause of the First Amendment which eventually emerged from protracted debate:

> Congress shall make no law respecting an establishment of religion or prohibiting the free exercise thereof.

This provision was later made binding on the states by the Fourteenth Amendment. There was no hair-splitting here — no tortuous agonizing over what did and did not constitute a church. There were no fine points as, for example, how completely a church institution must separate itself from a church in order not to be a church. There was a complete disassociation of the state's processes from the area of religion. Government was simply acknowledging that it had no competence here and that it proposed to keep out. Government would undertake to do nothing whatever about religion save to insure its free exercise.

There is no more definitive aspect of the authority of government than its power to tax. The entire governmental process in a real sense centers here. The power to tax is the essence of government. To exert this basic authority of government on behalf of the church is to end separation and move toward union at the most fundamental point. For government to use the taxing power on behalf of the church is to join the two. This is precisely what the

192

founding fathers thought they had avoided for all time when, after their extended debate and deliberation, they finally produced the religion clause of the First Amendment.

There exists today a gigantic conspiracy to scuttle this entire church-state arrangement and the great majority of its people are simply not aware of it. One day they will awaken and in great anger they will reverse the situation. This has frequently happened in the past and it will happen again.

Let us first assess the church-state trend from the political standpoint; then, second, from the standpoint of religion. What we see at this point is the emergence of the question of church school subsidies as a political issue. This is something the United States has not seen in more than a hundred years. For the most part, religious issues have not played any large role in American politics.

Today we see proposals for government aid to parochial schools being taken up as a specific political issue. Such proposals now become planks in the platforms of political parties and campaign fodder for political candidates. We are familiar with the Christian Democratic parties of Europe and Latin America. These are more properly Roman Catholic parties whose policies are generally oriented toward the denominational interests of that church — along with a generally conservative approach to political problems. In the United States, Roman Catholics have traditionally voted the Democratic ticket. The political machines which ran our big cities had a religio-ethnic orientation and were typically directed by bosses who were both Democrat and Catholic. There was close liaison between city hall and the diocese. There was such a thing as the Catholic vote and it was generally Democratic.

Today that is changing rapidly. As this is written, the Republicans are making a great pitch for the Catholic vote and apparently they are beginning to get a piece of it. A shift of the Catholic vote from Democratic to Republican was said to be a factor in the election of Richard Nixon over Hubert Humphrey in 1968. We can see this trend even more significantly in recent state elections. We see it above all in the use of the issue of government aid to parochial schools as a campaign lure to appeal to the Catholic vote. It is the Republicans who have now seized upon this legacy of LBJ. They are riding it hard in state elections and are preparing to use it as an issue in national elections as well. In the 1970 race for the Republican nomination for United States Senator, Governor James A. Rhodes sought to win over Robert Taft with a parochiaid appeal for the Catholic vote.

As noted previously, Rhodes, a Presbyterian, made state subsidies for parochial schools one of the salient features of his administration as governor. He used the considerable powers of a governor whose party has controlling majorities in both Houses to get what he wanted. There can be no doubt that this tactic appealed to the hierarchy who provided the most enthusiastic endorsements of his candidacy for the Republican nomination for United States Senator from Ohio.

Still, Rhodes lost the nomination to Robert Taft. It was close, but he lost. He lost, many believe, because of a miscalculation on the Catholic vote. While Rhodes got some of this vote, he did not get it all and the part he failed to get is as significant as the part he got. What Rhodes failed to realize is that today a considerable segment of the Catholic community no longer follows its priests blindly on the matter of denominational schools. Many Catholics today see no sense in continuing the separate schools of the denomination. Note, for example, the militant stand on this issue by the National Association of (Catholic) Laity. Such voters actually resented the Rhodes program of attempting to bribe Catholic voters and cast their ballots for his opponent. In addition, many priests oppose state aid to their schools because this may invite state control and dilute the religious teaching. This is opposition from an entirely different base but it is very formidable. It is a strong, conservative influence which fears that government subsidy will inevitably undermine the Catholic school as a religious force. The priest brothers, Casimir F. and Joseph A. Gierut of Bunker Hill, Illinois and Detroit, Michigan respectively, are representative of this group. There is also opposition to parochiaid by many religious and secular groups who believe it jeopardizes church-state separation.

In the New Jersey gubernatorial election of 1970, William Cahill, himself an Irish Catholic with eight children, wooed the Catholic vote for the Republican ticket somewhat more adroitly. At the eleventh hour of his campaign he suddenly came out for state aid to ease the burdens of the parochial schools. His Democratic opponent, William Meyner, was taken by surprise. He refused, however, to offer a counter bribe since he knew perfectly well the state would have no money to fund it. This fact did not bother Cahill who was elected and then found precisely that situation when he sought to make good on his campaign pledge. Governor Cahill pushed the bill through anyway, and it was immediately confronted with a court challenge.

There are other facets of the appeal of the Catholic vote. This is very much an appeal to the conservative side and we can see how it relates to the Republican southern strategy. The hope has never died there for some kind of formula for providing public support of private schools created to avoid racial integration. So Gov. Lester Maddox of Georgia constantly heralded the virtues of private schools and advocated a tuition grant program of public assistance to support them. This is the very direction the Republican strategy is now pointing and the reason for it is apparent: it is an appeal for the conservative and Catholic vote. Private schools to preserve racial segregation are burgeoning over the south. All they lack is a method of tax support to put them on a firm basis and it is possible that the tuition voucher program with which the Nixon Administration is now experimenting may be that method. We discussed the tuition voucher plan in Chapter 6. It is a good one since it can be advocated in an aura of impartiality, fairplay and freedom of choice. The student, or rather his parents, receive a tuition voucher for their child's education. This voucher can be cashed for tuition in any accredited school to which the student can gain admission. Theoretically, all schools receiving the grants would have to be open to students of all races and creeds and there would likely be some tokenism in this direction. But who can doubt that this program would end up doing just what it is supposed to do — provide public subsidy for religiously ,racially and ideologically segregated schools?

As we have seen, the OEO has already poured $196,313 into a study of the tuition voucher plan. The recommendation from the study is that $40 million more be invested in a five year experiment with the plan. Commenting on the proposal, Daniel Patrick Moynihan, Presidential counselor, stated that there was "nothing in the First Amendment that says we can't study" aid to nonpublic schools. The tuition voucher plan might well be the new stratagem for evading the application of the First Amendment stricture to federal grants for religious schools. As this was being written the OEO was initiating tuition voucher experiments in a number of communities widely scattered throughout the country.

One must keep in mind the definitive difference between *any* private school and the public school: the private school can pick and choose, excluding whom it will; the public school has to take everybody. Nothing that can be said about freedom of choice and competition in education and all the rest, can efface that distinction. When public funds are used to support schools whose students and teachers are selected on the basis of discriminations of various kinds, this merely exacerbates the differences in educational opportunity. It rewards the privileged and deprives the deprived. And it aids religion.

Whether it be by tuition vouchers, tax credits, or some other plan, the Nixon Administration sought to orient its strategy toward wider aid programs for church schools. In a major message on education delivered to the Congress on March 3, 1970, President Nixon pleaded the case of the church schools and directed the Presidential Commission on Education to develop "recommendations for achieving greater cooperation between public and nonpublic schools in furthering the education of all children." He spoke of the financial needs of the church schools and of the strain that would be imposed upon public facilities if all such institutions were to close. "The government," he said, "cannot be indifferent to the potential collapse of such schools." We have noted that the Commission, though badly divided on the subject, did recommend a variety of parochiaid schemes.

The direction of the Administration was shown by its fanfare announcing an Office of Education grant of $40,000 — not to students in schools, but to Roman Catholic schools in Los Angeles and San Francisco for special summer reading programs in 1970. To underscore the nature of the grants, they will include stipends of $75 a week to Roman Catholic nuns who will conduct the programs.

Thus it appeared that President Nixon was tilting his Administration in the direction of wider federal aid to church schools. This appeared to be another version of the bid for the Catholic vote. Perhaps it should more properly be called an appeal to a conservative consensus. For the conservative appeal in private and parochial school patronage has become very clear. It appeals to conservatives by enabling them to do what they have long wanted to do and to call it something else. It would enable them to maintain segregated schools serving the skimmed off, better students, and to do it with tax funds.

The forecast for New York State offered by *News Day* in its April 20, 1970, issue may be what we can expect generally:

> When this (church-state) issue was last before the voters in 1967 tensions among religious groups increased enormously. In a pluralistic society such inter-group fighting is dangerous because it destroys accustomed modes of accommodation. But if the public purse were ever fully opened to church schools, the condition would grow far more menacing. Then the debate would escalate into actual competition for state funds. For it is difficult to imagine one group standing by and watching another develop its institutions at public expense.
>
> This competitive menace is even more disturbing when its impact on the public schools is considered. At present, the state is unable to find the money adequately to finance public education. What happens when private and parochial schools can make a legitimate claim on the already insufficient pool of money? There is little question that the public schools would enter an era of decline. New York's lawmakers appear determined to open this Pandora's box.

It is sad that the church-state issue should have appeared in American politics in this form at this time. The result is bound to be divisive and the effect on religion itself unfortunate. This "thrust for subsidy" now being espoused by a particular candidate seeking to woo the Catholic vote will presently be opposed by another candidate. Here we find the church in a pitiable posture as it is supported and opposed by candidates in the political arena. This process cannot but degrade the ministry of the church as it is subjected to the rigors of political controversy. The church may well lose its struggle for public subsidy. If it does, it will look bad for having tried.

But there is always the possibility that the church may succeed in its ambition. This would be even worse. For the church would then be using the compulsion of government to exact support from the people. The church would be using official coercion to impose its burdens on the taxpayers who have already served notice that they do not want to carry them. This brings us to our assessment of the current church-state trend from the standpoint of religion.

Why have pressures from the church side suddenly zeroed in on the wall of separation between church and state, threatening to breach it irreparably? So far as elementary and secondary church schools are concerned, the pressures are being exerted almost solely by the Roman Catholic Church. In Michigan there has been some activity by the Christian Reformed Church. Occasionally a Jewish day school will evidence interest in government subsidy. Many Lutherans and Adventists operating church schools have disclaimed any interest in government aid and have made it clear that they would regard it as an intrusion on the private, independent character of their schools. Over-all, the pressure is Roman Catholic. Why is this?

Catholic leaders complain that their schools have been caught in the inflationary spiral and that they can no longer maintain them. It is evident, however, that the real problem runs much deeper. Certainly the Catholic schools are in decline. In 1970 the National Catholic Educational Association reports that Catholic enrollment in elementary and secondary schools in the United States declined by 750,000 in the last 5 years, with 500,000 of the decrease coming in 1968 and 1969. By 1972 the loss had topped a million. The report to the bishops in November, 1970 said that if the trend continues the peak enrollment of 1965 would be cut in half by 1975. "The emerging crisis in Catholic education," said one of the reports, "is a shortage of students." The recommendation was for a "home to home recruitment for increased attendance at Catholic schools."

Are Catholic contributions for schools declining? We have no way of knowing. For comprehensive, audited reports of income and assets and expenditures are usually not provided. It is ironical that while cries of dire need for public subsidy are regularly heard from the Catholic leaders, they seem to feel no obligation to let the public know what their situation really is. Louis R. Gary, author of the Gary Report to Governor Rockefeller's Fleishmann Commission in New York State, reports that "overall Catholic families contribute less than 2 per cent of their income to the parish church, and the rich contribute a far smaller proportion of their income than do the poor." (*Saturday Review*, July 22, 1972). It appears that many laymen have become dubious of the wisdom of trying to maintain a separate Catholic school system when Catholic leaders, by their own admission, are seeking to make their schools just like the public schools. But such opinion really has no way of being expressed and felt in the Catholic community where the hierarchy has traditionally made all the decisions. This explains why at the very time there is a crisis of confidence in Catholic schools, the pressure for public subsidy to these institutions has mounted to almost intolerable fury.

It should be pointed out that the parochial decline is almost exclusively a Catholic phenomenon. Other sectarian schools are multiplying and private schools of all kinds, save the Catholic, are on the increase. Adventists and Lutherans have steadily increased their schools during the period of Catholic decline. The problem is, obviously, one unique to the Catholics and we can quickly locate it. It is the decline of their corps of free teachers. In each of the past two years the Roman Catholic Church lost the services of thousands of nuns and brothers in the United States, most of whom were engaged in teaching at parochial schools. The church also lost about 3,000 priests in each of these years. Recruitment of future religious is down everywhere and seminaries and novitiates are being closed. This loss has had a profound impact on the denominational schools. A teaching nun receives only subsistence — about $2,000 per annum. But a lay teacher must be paid at least three times that figure. This, in a word, is the Catholic problem with their parochial schools. And this also explains why Catholic schools in the near future will cost just as much as public schools or any others. Apparently the Catholic hierarchy does not expect any relief from this situation — only that it will steadily worsen. We can anticipate, therefore, no diminution in clerical pressures for public subsidy. On the contrary, we can expect such pressures to become even more intense. The clergy will not voluntarily surrender their institutional domain but will, rather, exert every possible effort to retain it. As their donors fail, they will look increasingly to the taxpayers.

Does the Catholic Church really need tax money for its schools? Churches are not required by law to disclose their finances and some of the largest, like the Roman Catholic Church, do not. We do know that this church has vast assets. Its wealth in the United States totals more than $80 billion with about $54 billion of this in assessed valuation of tax-exempt property.[3] The $54 billion is the Catholic portion of the $102 billion total of religiously exempt property in the United States. In the *Catholic Directory* the listing of properties of the New York archdiocese alone takes up 29 pages, three columns to the page, of print so fine that it invites the use of a magnifying glass. The Boston archdiocese occupies 21 pages in the same manner. This, of course, does not include church-owned property on which taxes are paid. Nor does it include any of the commercial businesses and the hotels, apartment houses and retirement homes and stocks and bonds owned by the church. The annual income of this church from all sources is at least $13 billion. We are obviously dealing here with a wealthy and powerful entity.

Yet we have loud cries of poverty and earnest pleas that without prompt assistance from tax funds this church will have to give up at least some of its schools. The probable explanation is that the Roman Catholic Church is not suffering in its wealth and assets but is short of funds for current expenses. This church is somewhat in the position of a tycoon who owns a commercial complex, apartment houses, shopping centers and service stations but lacks ready cash. It might be wise to pull in at this point, to reduce the dimensions of the capital outlay. But the church is extremely reluctant to do this. Nor is it willing to put any of its capital funds into current expenditures of schools. Hence, its problems grow as do its demands on the taxpayers. Whether the Catholic Church is rich or poor, however, is really irrelevant to the subsidy issue. Our tradition in church and state has denied government subsidy to poor and rich churches alike.

Such pressures are denting and bending the wall of separation between church and state. Within the past decade we have witnessed the beginnings of a substantial and far-reaching change in the pattern of such relations which had obtained for a century-and-a half preceding. Because the change was called by different names few have recognized it. It has come about not by a dramatic repeal of the First Amendment nor, to this point, by any epochal change in companion provisions of state constitutions. The church is seeking its subsidies by means of a series of tricks or maneuvers in which the church-state provisions are simply being evaded.

What are some of these tricks? We stated them briefly in Chapter 2. Let us now examine them in detail. One was that while government could not subsidize church schools, it could aid the children in them. If pressed far enough and hard enough this could give away the entire case. For anything done for a school would certainly be of some benefit to the children in it. It could be argued, for example, that construction of modern, functional buildings by the state for the church would benefit the persons who used them. Child benefit in aid of persons within a denominational context and under its aegis is inevitably an institutional benefit. It is subsidy to a church.

Another trick is the one which says that the state can pay for the secular part of the instruction in religious schools. Here is presented the fiction that a church school neatly divides its program of instruction into two unequal divisions. One division comprising 90 to 95 per cent of the curriculum is secular. This is the basic reading, writing and arithmetic studies to which the compulsory requirements of the state are applicable. The other 5 to 10 per cent is a small addendum called religion which is added by the church in the form of a brief period each day. The theory here is that taxes can be used to support the great bulk of the church school teaching — all except the small portion that is specifically labeled religion.

The gimmick overlooks the entire nature of the church school, its whole purpose and modus operandi. The typical church school is owned and managed by clergy with much of its teaching provided by clerically garbed religious. Its highest authorities have repeatedly asserted that the purpose of the school is denominational and that it seeks to permeate the curriculum with its doctrine. It exists to segregate its votaries from the rest of the community and to recruit from among them members of its clergy and religious orders. Furthermore, the church schools carefully select their clientele, eliminating delinquents and problems and low aptitudes, as well as those unable to pay the fees. These are private, sectarian schools. In no proper sense are they public schools qualifying for tax support. Even if we accept this contention on its face, however, we cannot escape the fact that government aid to the secular teaching in a

201

church school is a basic form of aid to that school. What, indeed, could be more essential to the success and survival of a church school than good secular teaching? This is the cornerstone of the school. Without this there would be no patrons.

There was the plea that since the state imposed certain records and requirements on parochial schools, such as counting the number of students, the state could compensate them for fulfillment. This one is obviously absurd. It could bring every private group and citizen in the country into court claiming that if, for example, the government required that their buildings should have protection against fire, the government would have to provide the buildings. Such a doctrine would make government regulation of anything possible.

Widely current today is the plea that government can subsidize church schools in a permissible manner if it uses the parents of students as conduits to channel the money into the school. That is, the state can convey a cash advantage to the parent of a parochial school pupil either by reducing his income tax or by paying him a tuition allowance directly. This is obvious circumvention of the law; the parents are no more than conduits for the aid. So the courts have already found, and so, we believe, the Supreme Court will find.

There was the ruse that aid to churches and church schools was essential to winning the war against poverty. The facts are that there was nothing the churches did which could not have been done as well or better by public agencies.

One of the oldest claims advanced for aid to church-related institutions was that such aid would buttress national defense. There was no substance to this. While government aid to church institutions might have resulted in some remote and incidental benefit to defense, there was certainly nothing that could not have been accomplished by public institutions and agencies.

Another device which may yet open the way for a substantial and functional union of church and state is the plea that government can subsidize churches in the performance of secular functions if the effect of the function is on which conveys a secular benefit and neither advances nor inhibits religion. Under this banner the church could be entirely supported by taxes save possibly for such items as books of worship and altar hangings.

Yet another rationale dear to the heart of legislators is that it is cheaper for government to hire and use the church for certain services in welfare and education than to perform them directly through the government bureaucracy. While there might be some initial justification for this, the long-run prognosis is definitely negative. For what happens is that we develop not one immense bureaucracy but two — both supported by the taxpayers.

The greatest hoax of all in terms of the numbers it has deceived is the one which asserts that it is cheaper for the government to provide some aid to parochial schools than to see these schools close and have their pupils transferred into the public system. There are several things wrong with this argument. The Catholic school closings, as we have seen, are due not to a shortage of money but to a shortage of students. Non tuition and low tuition Catholic schools are closing at about the same rate as high tuition schools. The decline in Catholic enrollments will continue at about the same rate, we are told, whether government subsidies are given to these schools or not. The Fleishmann report in New York State, for example, found that Catholic schools there will experience a 42 per cent drop in enrollment in the 1970's whether they get substantial state aid or not.

Furthermore, the public school enrollment is also declining, particularly at the elementary level. The *Occupational Outlook* published by the Bureau of Labor Statistics reveals that the birthrate fell steadily during the 1960's and that the decline is even more abrupt in the 1970's. The day of rapidly expanding school population is over — parochial or public. The decline has already begun. Under such a condition, with vacant seats and rooms showing up in many areas, the economies of management would obviously be better served by absorbing the parochial students into the public system. This point has been hammered home in the Gary Report to the Fleishmann Commission and also in a study of Catholic school closings, *When Parochial Schools Close, A Study in Private and Public School Finance,* by Martin A. Larson, published by Robert B. Luce, Inc., Washington, D.C. The Gary Report estimated the savings which would result from absorption of parochial school students into the public system at $415 million in operating costs alone during the 1970's.

As a result of these various ruses, flimsy as most of them are, the church-state provisions are being circumvented. We are witnessing a de facto interlocking of church and state. This is an effort to achieve what the founding fathers in their deep understanding of history had sought to avoid, a functional and financial union of state and church. The courts have now become almost the sole barrier against this disaster, but the courts must have popular support if they are to continue to hold the line.

What, then, can we anticipate in church-state relations in the 1970's and 1980's?

A decade ago, as the first proposals for federal aid to church schools were beginning to gain favor in Congress, the writer made a statement as to the direction it seemed to him such proposals would take us. That statement which appeared in *Government and Education, the Thirty-Fifth Discussion and Debate Manual,* 1961, can be appropriately quoted at this point:

What is significant about this legislation is the direction in which it points. What is proposed here is a drastic revision of our whole traditional public policy in regard to church institutions. We shall have commenced to move from churches as free, voluntary associations toward churches that are ironed into the operations of government. The end of this road is the complete financing of church schools from tax funds. This, in turn, points to the fragmentation of our educational system and the fragmentation of our culture.

We see a change in the direction of tax support of the church and away from voluntary support. Government aid to the churches increased steadily through the 1960s. The trend continues. The churches' tax-exempt land and wealth have also increased. It has been estimated that churches now receive annually from the many programs of government aid available to them about $7 billion; also that over-all church wealth is increasing at about the rate of $5 billion annually.[4] The church-owned corpus of tax-exempt real estate may now comprise 10 per cent of the whole.[5]

Government subsidies to church institutions need to be examined in connection with the religious tax exemption. It has been argued, and with some logic, that exemption from tax for houses of worship is necessary to the free exercise of religion. But this basic form of religious tax exemption has steadily expanded until it has come to include much besides the actual house of worship. In many states the rectories or parsonages housing the clergy are also exempt. Sometimes revenue-producing real estate has been exempted as well. The exemption has been extended at times to highly lucrative housing projects of the church and even to the profits of commercial business operated by a church or leased back by the church, business which is quite unrelated to religious functions.

Changes in the Internal Revenue Code approved by Congress and signed into law by President Nixon late in 1969 do impose a federal tax on profits of the unrelated business of churches when purchased with borrowed funds. But for such businesses owned by the church as of May 26, 1969, a five-year shelter is provided. Again, a church can purchase real estate with the announcement that it intends to build a house of worship on the property. It can hold the property, enjoying all income from it tax-free for 15 years and then dispose of it without a capital gains levy. Other nonprofit corporations are limited to a 10 year period within which they must build and are also subjected to a neighborhood test. This is, their proposed site must be adjacent to their present headquarters. Not so the church, which can acquire its proposed site anywhere.

The exemptions and preferred treatment in tax matters for both the churches and their clergy are beyond the scope of this book. They are numerous and imposing. One of the most important preferences given the church is that which accords religious orders the same tax immunities as a church. Such an immunity provides a tax shelter for billions of dollars in property, other assets and income. Most remarkable of all perhaps is that the law makes churches or associations of churches immune to financial disclosure. In the ordinary course, no reports of their holdings or reports are required. Some data may be asked of them but only in a case where gross chicanery is suspected, and then only in connection with the particular item in question. Such an investigation can only originate with an official not lower than a district director. Churches are not even required to disclose their finances to their own members and some of the big ones like the Roman Catholic and The Church of Jesus Christ of Latter Day Saints do not.

Thus it can be seen that the simple tax exemption for a modest house of worship has burgeoned into virtual establishment of religion. The favored tax position of the churches is an irresistible stimulant to their wealth. Tax exemption enables the churches to expand their domain with scarcely any theoretical limitation. There is no between-the-generations divestiture for the church. It just goes on accumulating more and more property, more and more wealth.

Only one thing is lacking to perfect this picture of clerical aggrandizement: that is government subsidy for the church. Now we see that this, too, is being arranged by means of a variety of tricks and ruses. The religious exemptions, buttressed by the massive subsidies which government is now pouring into the churches, are building them into a religious establishment of awesome proportions. The churches are getting it both ways — through tax exemption and through government subsidy. All that remains for the completion of a familiar cycle which history has so often recorded is for this state-church combine to become oppressive of the people. That, too, now seems to be indicated as taxpayers are coerced into paying for the programs of the church.

President Ulysses S. Grant, speaking in 1875, warned the nation of the perils that could accrue from a burgeoning of the tax-exempt wealth of churches:

> In 1850 . . . church property in the United States which paid no tax . . . amounted to about $84 million. In 1860, the amount had doubled; in 1875 it is about $1 billion. . . . So vast a sum receiving all the protection and benefits of government without bearing its proportion of the burdens and expenses of the same, will not be looked upon acquiescently by those who have to pay the taxes. . . . there is scarcely a limit to the wealth that may be acquired by corporations, religious or otherwise, if allowed to retain real estate without taxation. The contemplation of so vast a property as here alluded to without taxation may lead to sequestration, without constitutional authority and through blood.
>
> I would suggest the taxation of all property, whether church or corporation. . . .

The danger President Grant saw was in the burgeoning tax-exempt domain of the churches. What if, in addition to this, he were to contemplate vast sums paid by government in direct and indirect subsidies to the churches? He would no doubt be convinced that the evil day he had foreseen had finally come to pass.

The spectacular rise of government subsidies to the church has been accompanied by a decline in voluntary giving. The drive to obtain even larger grants from this source will no doubt accelerate the process. While there are a number of factors involved in the decline of church giving, one of the big ones has to be state subsidies. When Stetson University, a Baptist institution in Florida, agreed to accept federal grants more than 60 churches promptly cut off their donations to the school. When public financing enters the picture, voluntary gifts can be expected to decline. This has been happening to all the major religious denominations. A church which is joined with the state or inter-functions with the state tends to lose its power of attraction for the people. The reason for this is that under such conditions the people associate the church with the image of coercion which belongs to the state. The decline in the collection plate is a predictable outcome.

The Board of Christian Education of the United Presbyterian Church, U.S.A. announced that its 1970 budget would have to be trimmed by nearly $1 million because of a decline in contributions. The retrenchment includes a cut of $470,000 in church subsidies to 46 Presbyterian-related colleges. The Episcopal Bishop of San Francisco announced a cutback in the diocesan program because of declining donations. The Episcopal diocese of Hawaii reported that as a result of declining income it would seek to develop a commercial high-rise complex on its property in downtown Honolulu. A committee reported that development of extremely valuable parcels was needed to keep the diocese operating in the black.

The Long Island diocese of this denomination reported on May 19, 1970, that for the past two years it had contributed $175,000 toward missions. In 1970, however, this would have to be cut to $50,000 because of declining donations. Of 114 parishes 45 paid only part or nothing at all on their missionary pledges. Long Island Diocesan Bishop Richard B. Martin denounced "the deliberate withholding from the missionary operations of the diocese and the general church."

The United Presbyterian Church, U.S.A. contemplated a decline of $5 million in benevolent giving over a one year period. The Roman Catholic Church generally continues its policy of financial secrecy, but its clergy constantly reiterate the hard up theme. This applies particularly to their schools which they say they may have to discontinue altogether if they cannot obtain government subsidies.

At the United Methodist General Conference of 1970 it was announced that a number of its agencies would have to absorb a 6 per cent cutback and the denomination's contributions to the American Bible Society was to be cut $100,000. The Rev. R. Bricker Gibson, pastor of Chestnut Street Congregational Church, Worcester, Massachusetts, reported that statewide mission collections for his denomination, The United Church of Christ, had dropped $110,000 in 1969 over the preceding year. The Southern California Arizona Conference of the United Methodist Church reported a decline in donations of 10 per cent in 1969 from the 1968 figure. The Lutheran Church in America announced a 1969-1972 cutback in missions due to falling income. Virtually all of the larger church groups reported a decrease in contributions. As the use of tax funds for church support continues to increase, we can anticipate that voluntary donations will continue to decline.

Support of American church budgets is suffering all along the line. The National Council of Churches is hurting as is its sister group, the World Council of Churches. Many United States denominations failed to meet their commitments to the World Council in 1969. United States churches failed by $52,000 to meet their obligation of $709,515. The United States branch of the World Council ran a deficit of $11,755 on a total budget of $112,550 and anticipates a much greater deficit in 1970. In 1969 the National Council failed to raise its operating budget of $27.3 million by $1.8 million. It avoided a deficit of this size by cutting back its program during the year. The trend of declining support continued into 1970 and there were further cutbacks in departmental budgets.

Most major church groups have recorded drops in membership in recent years. The United Methodist Church, the nation's second largest Protestant denomination, reported a decline of over 200,000 in 1969. In fact, this church has registered a loss in membership for five consecutive years. Other Protestant denominations, with the exception of the Southern Baptist, the Mormon, and the Lutheran, Missouri Synod, also reported losses.

It is interesting that the Church of Jesus Christ of Latter Day Saints (Mormon), one of the two religious bodies in the nation which continues to report substantial gains in membership, has steadfastly refused government subsidy for its schools. The other, the Seventh-day Adventist, has never accepted government subsidy for its schools. Yet another, the Southern Baptist, has exhibited strong resistance to government subsidy for its institutions.

Others have indicated steady shrinkage in membership. The 1970 *Yearbook of American Churches* showed that in addition to the United Methodist, losses in membership had been recorded by the Episcopal, United Presbyterian, U.S.A., United Presbyterian U.S., Christian (Disciples of Christ), American Baptist and Lutheran Church in America. This source also reports an over-all decline of church membership in relation to the general population. In five years this figure had declined from 64.4 per cent in 1964 to 63.1 per cent in 1970.

Even the Roman Catholic Church, the nation's largest, has succumbed to the downward trend. According to the 1970 *Official Catholic Directory,* that church declined in all the following categories: members, priests, nuns, brothers, adult and infant baptisms, schools, students in Catholic schools and houses of worship. The Catholic population had recorded a gain in the United States every year until 1970. There was a decline of 6,236 in the number of sisters, many of them teachers in Catholic schools. There was a decline of 9,174 in the number of sisters during the preceding year of 1969, making a total of 15,410 for the two years. Catholic schools at all levels showed a substantial decline in enrollment.

One of the most sensational aspects of the Roman Catholic decline was pinpointed by the *National Catholic Reporter,* May 29, 1970. The *Reporter* pointed to the decline of 313,252 students in Catholic elementary and secondary schools, then went on to the figure of 313,414 fewer students enrolled for parish instruction in religion. Said the *Reporter:* "The figures seem to say that more than 600,000 fewer Catholic young people are going without any formal religious education than in the previous year." (This inference was, however, denied by church officials.)

A no less predictable result is the decline in church attendance. In 1969 the percentage of Americans who attend church regularly dropped to 63 per cent for Catholics and 37 per cent for Protestants, a low for the decade. In each of the years 1968 and 1969 over 3,000 Protestant ministers in the United States left their pulpits for secular employment, many of them, incidentally, with the Office of Economic Opportunity. The corresponding figure for Catholic priests was about the same — 3,000 departures for each of the two years. This, according to a survey conducted by the Rev. James J. Gill, a Jesuit priest who serves on the faculty of Harvard University. Again, one of the apparent reasons for the defections was the availability of good jobs with the OEO.

The Episcopal Board for Theological Education recommended closing of six of the eleven theological seminaries operated by this denomination. The reasons: declining contributions and declining enrollments. Other seminaries, both Protestant and Catholic, were closing while still others were effecting mergers to continue in operation. These defections and declines reflect to a certain extent a growing disillusionment with the church. Some of this disenchantment in both pulpit and pew can be traced to the increasing penchant of the church for the state's financing and sponsorship. The thrust of conviction so basic to the virility of the religious enterprise is clearly on the wane. The new church-state entente does not arrest but markedly hastens this decline.

Most remarkable of all is the condition of the church in the popular estimate. It is not so much that people think badly of the church; they just do not think well of it. A sampling of opinion taken by Gallup in 1969 indicated that the number of Americans who thought that "religion as a whole is losing its influence" stood at 75 per cent. Thirteen years earlier only 14 per cent had thought so.

This total result is at least partially due to the inter-functioning of state and church and especially the willingness of the church to use tax funds. A church quickly loses the affection of the people when they are taxed to support it and likely their respect as well. People do not like to be taxed at all. But there is no surer way to stir their animosity than to tax them at the point of religion. They may put up with it in sullen silence and that is about what the church which accepts tax support will get. That, or something more violent.

Another aspect of the developing union of church and state is the ambition of the state to use the church for the achievement of purposes which are regarded as public and secular in nature. Government today is participating in the affairs of churches and churches are participating in the affairs of government. Their goal has been defined as one — the welfare of the people. In the pursuit of welfare it has been deemed sound procedure for government to hire the church and use it for the performance of certain tasks. If there were no public agencies available (such as public schools) to perform these functions, one could understand the necessity of hiring the churches. But with myriad public agencies at hand, the recourse to the churches must appear gratuitous. The goal is not so much to purchase service as to confer subsidy. How Methodist leaders are groping toward this position is demonstrated by the Report of a Study Commission of the United Methodist Church dealing with Church-Government Relations for the General Conference of 1968. The report says that "in the case of church-related educational institutions, the cooperation (between church and state) referred to may take the support of governmental support of special purpose educational programs that bear a clear relation to a legitimate objective of public policy."

The willingness of the church to be hired by the state does not help its image. The more it continues the more the church is made to appear as a mere tool of the state. The church loses its stature as an entity in its own right and becomes a tail to the state's kite. The decline of the church has been ascribed to the secularization of our culture. A prime factor in this process is that the supposed archenemy of secularism — the church — has itself been secularized. This has come about in large part through its interlocking and inter-functioning with the state.

The English Bishop John A.T. Robinson in describing the condition of the Church of England might have been referring to that of the church in America as well. It has "become heavily institutionalized with a crushing investment in maintenance. . . . It is absorbed in problems of supply and preoccupied with survival. The inertia of the machine is such that the financial allocations, the legalities, the channels of organization, the attitudes of mind, are all set in the direction of continuing and enhancing the status quo."[6]

Surely the church's increasing involvement with the state has aggravated this condition. There is far too close a relationship between our political and religious institutions. Of all the ties between them the financial are most significant. For many organic interrelationships result from these. The reception of tax funds by the church leads to an inevitable participation in each other's affairs by state and church.

The political orientation of the church toward the state has added to its wealth and power. The increasing use of tax funds for the church has built up its institutional strength. It has also encouraged massive forays into unrelated business — i.e., business not related to the normal functions of a church. Despite the attempt at reform which we have described, the tax laws still retain many tax shelters for the church — enough, certainly, for it to continue to augment its economic power.

In the shift from voluntaryism to coercion in the matter of church finance we would normally expect government to assume a larger role in church management. This would be on the old theory that he who pays the piper calls the tune. To a certain extent this has happened. We have seen how under the Horace Mann doctrine of the Maryland case the colleges have been rather systematically diluting their clerical control. Yet in many instances this has been a nominal dilution rather than one of substance. It has eliminated the religious emphasis, but not the de facto clerical management. Some of the window dressing has been shifted but the church tends to remain in charge. This is to say that the government hands over the money along with certain broad guidelines for its expenditure. The church takes it from there. If there is some crass, overt violation of the guidelines, government might react to it. But other than this, the church simply proceeds on its own and does as it wills.

What really happens in this kind of transaction? What happens is that the coercive power of the state enters the shell of the church institution. The state supplies the sinews of power and money to a church which is unsupported and unloved by the people. The church moves to a higher level of incompetence. No matter what splendid service it may be alleged to perform, its performance under these conditions will not be appreciated. Here, in fact, we have the ingredients of clericalism and the anticlericalism which it invariably

212

provokes. We have here the commencement of a process which may possibly develop as it has so often in the past. From coldness and indifference, the people turn to resentment and anger, and the fires of anticlericalism burn again.

We are presently in the stage of coldness and indifference. The people do not attend; the contributions decline. What we should expect to see in this process is what we do see — the steady deterioration of the churches as an effective spiritual force. And what is even more significant for our discussion here, we see a diminution in the church's power of attraction. As public concerns and functions take over, the church loses its charisma. This might ordinarily occasion no great disruption. The trouble is that the people always expect more of the church and when they do not get it resentment rises. They do not want the church to be official and political, vying with other government bureaucracies. The want it to be something special and different. When it turns out to be more of the same they turn against it in a kind of hostility unmatched in other cases. We see, therefore, two trends: (1) The church is wealthier and more politically potent than ever before; (2) The Church becomes religiously ineffective and alienated from the people even as it effectively works its will with the state. It seems likely that both these trends will continue.

What we see emerging is a hybrid creation, an inchoate amalgam of government and religion with the vices and weaknesses of both and the virtues of neither. The churches gave a glorious account of themselves when they were pioneering and improvising in projects that would fall or stand on the basis of their own inherent worth. Their work in missions, in healing, welfare and education was often a thrust of inventiveness. With some kind of ingenious cut-and-paste improvisation the church would show how a much needed job could be done. Eventually, the ponderous bureaucracy of governmental procedure would begin to catch on and take over. By that time the church would be pioneering somewhere else.

What we are now doing is to add the church to the government bureaucracy with its most strenuous job that of wheedling its annual stipend from the legislators and administrators. It is a now you see it, now you don't proposition so far as church and state are concerned. The church institution, as in the case of the college, becomes a quasi public institution. Yet it retains some of the trappings of the church and certain vestigal aspects of its direction and control. Now the same process commences in the schools belonging to the church. Church administrators vie with one another in their denials of any effective religious atmosphere or teaching. Government administrators are solemnly assured that these schools are just as secular in their teaching as are public schools, and they can be hired the same as any others to carry out the compulsory education program of the state.

In welfare operations the church abandons its innovative role and merges with the state's bureaucracy. The clergy become agents of the state quite as surely as police and firemen, and parish organizations become little Tammany Halls. Thousands of clergymen formalize the merger by joining the state's bureaucracy and receiving their pay from it. What is most depressing about this process is the apparent willingness of the church administrators to enter upon it. Foy Valentine, executive secretary of the Christian Life Commission of the Southern Baptist Convention, has given a morbid but accurate description of it:

> . . . This willingness to be used, the neurotic prostitution of ourselves. . . . There are numerous indications that both the national and the state governments are more and more looking on the churches as another of their numerous resources. While this attitude may be both natural and inevitable for the government, it is a tragic phenomenon to see the churches playing along in this deadly game. If they do not maintain their freedom, they cannot maintain their usefulness either to the Kingdom of God or the kingdom of men.[7]

But let a federal program of financial aid to church institutions commence and the line promptly forms to the left. The church leadership is quick to join up and take what it is being offered. Wherever and whenever the state patronage is available this seems to be true. This may be due, in part, to a desire to serve. But there is another factor as well. This is due, in part, to the love of money. The Pope once remarked of Calvin: "The power of that heretic is that he is in-

214

different to money." Few are. And it matters not whether they button their collars behind or before.

Under such circumstances the church ceases to be the church. It becomes something else. The prophetic voice of the church which in other times served the state so well is now silenced. The church is no longer critic of the state. It is a part of the state. As time goes on what gets attention and emphasis in the church is precisely those programs which are subsidized by the state. The clergy get into politics, lobbying defensively to keep their benefits. What might have begun as a fine, charitable endeavor ends up as a clerical incubus. The church becomes not a burden-bearer but a burden to be borne.

Of course this is not altogether true. Two denominations, the Southern Baptist and the Seventh-day Adventist, have been most successful among principal Protestant groups in resisting the financial subsidy and management of the state. Their record is by no means spotless. Baptists have succumbed here and there and the Adventists found the plenitude of subsidies available for their massive hospital program more than they could resist. These denominations stand out, however, not alone in their relatively high resistance to the engulfment, but in their serious recognition of the problem. At least they knew what was happening to them. For two decades and more their leadership has conducted thorough discussions of the problem. Not, perhaps, at the administrative level of these denominations, but certainly in the rank and file of their membership, a strong body of opinion supports strict separation of church and state.

It is not a coincidence that these denominations have continued to demonstrate virility while others have gone into decline. These denominations have been among the last to feel the secular slowdown which now afflicts the entire religious enterprise. Their relatively strong stand on the separation of church and state has done much more than help their image. It has kept the muscles firm and accentuated the reliance of these votaries upon their own efforts and the help of their God. State aid enfeebles; self reliance and faith empower.

Now, alas, we encounter an almost irresistible kind of pressure which operates to dissolve support of church-state separation among these groups. This is the competitive factor. The story is told of an ancient Christian hermit whose saintliness had won him wide renown. The man could handle any temptation with ease. He was out of this world. Finally, the matter came to the attention of the devil himself who devised a strategy of entrapment. He greeted the hermit with the remark: "I hear your brother has just been appointed bishop of Alexandria." The hermit turned pale. That got him; the competitive angle was too much!

Baptists and Seventh-day Adventists watch the other groups spreading their institutions in burgeoning splendor, far and wide. That gets them, for they know very well that they are paying for part of this in their taxes. Why, therefore, should they not be getting *their* share? Church people are just as human as others. They enjoy seeing massive buildings with their denominational name across the door. There is a prestige that accompanies institutional spread and few are impervious to its lure. How many times I have heard the remark: "Why should the Catholics get all the money when we are paying, too?"

Human nature being as it is, we can anticipate that these feelings will become stronger and that within the foreseeable future most church institutions and programs will be financed by the state. An astonishing characteristic of this development is that many church leaders of virtually all the denominations fail to see here any danger to the church. They speak of the growing church-state alignment as ushering in a brave, new day and they refer with high enthusiasm to an era of cooperation between church and state for the achievement of human good. That is to say that what will surely dilute and erode the moral influence of the church they see as desirable. This can only be described as another manifestation of a peculiar form of occupational blindness which has overtaken the clergy so frequently in the past.

Perhaps the devil is at work here! Again he shows them "all the kingdoms of the world and the glory of them."[8] He shows them what others are doing. Eventually they accept the proferred emoluments and patronage. Feelings of shame and compromise are suffused in solemn assurances that this is a new day and it is desirable that church and state end their separation and begin an era of cooperation. It would be hard to conceive of a strategy more demonically

216

successful in undermining and destroying the church than this one. It has now moved far toward its triumph and there is all too little evidence of any counter force rising to check its erosive power.

The results of this demonic gambit are two-fold. Both church and state suffer. The church is "un-Christed" so as to speak and is sapped of its religious significance. Indeed, those who, like the devil, have it in for the church could do no better than to arrange for vast government subsidies and the generous admixtures of public management which naturally accompany them. There is no surer way than this to do the church in. But the state suffers scarcely less. For it is deprived of the presence of the church in its prophetic role. When the state needs the voice of the church and listens for it, all it hears is its own voice. When the state seeks to dialogue with the church it finds that it is only talking to itself. The two have become one. The state has lost the church when it needed it most.

There is yet another ominous aspect of this developing pattern. The church seizes this moment of its greatest wealth and power to mount an all-out attack on the separation of church and state. It does what comes naturally; it uses its wealth and power to get more wealth and power. As we have seen, when state constitutions are to be revised, the church is at the head of the line seeking changes which will enable it to draw tax support. And it is churchmen who today beseige state legislatures to pass unconstitutional bills for the benefit of their institutions.

The great merger proceeds apace. It is being accomplished by a series of simplistic ruses most of them so patent as to be laughable. Executive, legislative and judiciary of the civil arm vie with churchmen in supplying the rationale. A disastrous denouement looms because few can grasp what is really happening and those who understand do not seem to care. We move toward a powerful, wealthy and totally secularized church formally and morally bound to a state whose secular aspirations it fully shares. This arrangement is not something bright and new; it is something old and drab. It is the dismal, discredited thing that history has recorded so often.

Will this combination now become oppressive, thus completing the cycle? The burgeoning of tax-exempt land and wealth of the church buttressed with vast exactions from the taxpayers point in this direction. This has happened before. It happened in France in

217

the eighteenth century; in England and Germany in the sixteenth; in Italy in the nineteenth; and in Russia and Mexico in the twentieth. In all of these situations the clerical cycle was completed in oppression of the people. Such oppression drew an appropriate anti-clerical reaction. Whether there is sufficient health in the churches and in the political process to resist these trends and to take corrective action is problematical. From time to time we do see some signs of awakening within the churches and an occasional feeble ray of awareness on the civil side. In the rare instances when they are permitted an expression of opinion, the people show a sound instinct. At the moment, however, such signs of promise are engulfed by a driving consensus of clergy and civil officials moving in the other direction. It is the weight of public opinion which in the final analysis will determine the outcome.

Notes

1. Padover, Saul K., *The Complete Jefferson*. Duell, Sloan & Pearce. New York. 1943, pp. 518-519.

2. Quoted in Dawson, J.M., *America's Way in Church. State and Society*. MacMillan Co., New York, 1953, p. 69

3. See Larson, Martin A. and Lowell, C. Stanley, *Praise the Lord for Tax Exemption*. Robert B. Luce, Inc., Washington, D.C., 1969, pp. 35-38

4. *Ibid.*

5. *Ibid.*, p.35

6. *Christianity Today*. April 10, 1970

7. Valentine, Foy, *The Cross in the Market Place*. Word Books, Waco, Texas, 1966, p.49

8. Matthew 6:8 (R.S.V.)

INDEX

222

town U. gets $8½ million 92